Birth of a Base - MacDill Field

1939 - 1941

Technical Sergeant Blaze E. Lipowski, USAF Retired

authorHOUSE®

AuthorHouse™
1663 Liberty Drive
Bloomington, IN 47403
www.authorhouse.com
Phone: 1-800-839-8640

© 2013 Technical Sergeant Blaze E. Lipowski, USAF Retired. All rights reserved.

No part of this book may be reproduced, stored in a retrieval system, or transmitted by any means without the written permission of the author.

Published by AuthorHouse 3/27/2013

ISBN: 978-1-4817-2993-2 (sc)
ISBN: 978-1-4817-2994-9 (e)

Any people depicted in stock imagery provided by Thinkstock are models, and such images are being used for illustrative purposes only.
Certain stock imagery © Thinkstock.

This book is printed on acid-free paper.

Because of the dynamic nature of the Internet, any web addresses or links contained in this book may have changed since publication and may no longer be valid. The views expressed in this work are solely those of the author and do not necessarily reflect the views of the publisher, and the publisher hereby disclaims any responsibility for them.

PREFACE

During my twenty years as an Air Force photographer, I spent time at some of the most historic Air Force Bases of the 20th century such as Lowery (Colorado), Langley (Virginia), Clark (Philippines), March (California) and finally MacDill (Florida). At the time, I did not realize the historical significance of these bases.

History held little interest for me until I was stationed at Charleston Air Force Base (AFB), South Carolina with the 1st Combat Camera Squadron. It wasn't until I took my first tour of Ft Sumter and listened to the park ranger's speech while I viewed the ruins around me that I realized there were once men behind those cannons firing back across the water to the union soldiers that were firing on them and attacking the fort. I started to imagine the men running around frantically, reloading those cannons, returning fire in their union uniforms and yelling for more ammunition. It played out like a mini-movie in my mind, giving me a chill afterwards. As horrific as it must have been, I found it amazing thinking of what was considered the "modern" technology of the times versus the technology of today.

As I toured the fort, I viewed drawings of the fort as it stood three stories tall and was under fire. I've seen photos taken of the fort in the aftermath of the battle which left it in ruins. There were many questions that I had after seeing those graphics and photos. I was amazed by the insight someone had to draw and take photos of, possibly not knowing what a historic information piece it will be in years to come.

On the boat ride back I began to regret my free time spent at Langley, my first duty station, and that I did not learn more about the base I spent two years at and how much I missed. I regretted not taking the tours of Williamsburg and learning more about its multiple places in history. Ever since that day, every place that I visit that has a historical significance, I try to learn more about it and ask myself: "What was it like?"; "How did this come about?"; "Who was here?"

My last years in the Air Force were spent at MacDill AFB, Florida. I had previously passed through MacDill in 1993 on my way to my new duty station at the U.S. Embassy in Mogadishu, Somalia via CENTCOM. Much had changed from what I remembered of the base from years ago. After a year being stationed at MacDill the base commander at the time, Col Robert D Thomas, tasked the newly assigned base historian Mr. William Polson, to collect photographs of all the commanders of the 6th as well as the commanders of MacDill for display in the headquarters building. Mr. Polson needed assistance in obtaining these photographs, so I was given the assignment after I expressed interest in the project. Shortly after, I had travel orders to Maxwell AFB, Alabama to obtain the required photographs from the Air Force Historical Research Agency (AFHRA).

After having a few volumes of information pulled to be researched for photographs, I came across a simple 8x10 yellowed page booklet held together by a simple metal clip. On the upper right hand corner it was stamped "To be returned to the AAF Historical Office, 23 May 1939-7 Dec 1941". On the bottom was stamped "Declassified 30 Sept 1959".

I breezed through a few pages, only to find myself lost in the story that unfolded. This coverless booklet which I held in my hands was the very first history report of Southeastern Air Base at Catfish Point in Tampa, Florida. Instead of reading like a history report, the booklet read more like a diary. As in that first visit to Fort Sumter all those years ago, I again in my mind envisioned the very first history officer, 2nd Lt John R. Jones, behind his typewriter. Perhaps he smoked a cigarette while he pecked away quickly at the typewriter keys while in his Army Air Force uniform. There wasn't any correction paper in the 1940's nor were there computers with word processors and the convenience of a backspace key to erase mistakes. I noticed there were few errors in this report, but the few that he made were easily forgiven.

With all this said, I invite you to travel back in time to 1939 through1941, to a time where one of the world's most important Air Force Bases was a barren waste land filled with rattlesnakes and trees. Travel back to a time where nothing was wasted and everything was used. Encounter Air Power figures that have rightfully left their mark in history, such as General Henry H. Arnold and General Clarence Tinker's command and fate during WWII. I hope you will find this as fascinating as I did when I first looked through the pages of a simple typewritten booklet.

I have kept the text of this book as true to form as it was found. Please keep in mind the time era and the social norms of the day. The photographs that are included in this book were ones that I located at AFHRA and the MacDill's base history office or that I purchased. Thank you, and enjoy.

NOTE FROM HISTORIAN

This book chronicles the beginning of MacDill Field, Florida in the two years before America's entrance into World War II. It covers the period from September 1939 until December 1941. Within this relatively short time, the 6,000 acres of sandy terrain, scrub brush, and rattlesnakes on Tampa's inter-bay peninsula transformed into the principle air field in the Southeast for training bomber crews. Later, many thousands of America's best and brightest young men would pass through MacDill's gates. They would quickly learn to fly and operate one of several types of bombers – perhaps, the B-17 "Flying Fortress" or the difficult-handling B-26 "Marauder" nicknamed the "Widowmaker" – and then quickly move on to another location, eventually destined for the deadly fight raging over Europe's skies.

Within these pages, you'll find references to many people, some famous and many anonymous, who helped shape the history of MacDill, as well as the U.S. Air Force. Some of these names are well known in Air Force and military circles. Herein is Colonel Clarence Tinker. An airman of Osage Indian ancestry, Tinker quickly turned MacDill from a fledgling air field into a training base for the bombers flying against Nazi Germany, before perishing in an attack at the Battle of Midway. Here too you'll find the first post surgeon, Colonel Malcolm Grow. He was one of the very few American officers to have served with the Russians during World War I, and later became the Air Force's first Surgeon General. Also passing through these pages: General Henry H. "Hap" Arnold, the only five-star General of the Air Force, and First Lieutenant John "Killer" Kane, who led the 98th Bomb Group "Pyramiders" in the "Operation Tidal Wave" attack against the oil refineries of Ploesti, Romania in 1943.

Blaze Lipowski's reprint not only documents the people who served at MacDill during this time, it was compiled and written by them also. No attempt has been made to rewrite the history or reinterpret their intents. This stands as a faithful reproduction of the official Air Force record (the original document can be found in the archives of the Air Force Historical Research Agency at Maxwell Air Force Base). However, MacDill's first history has been tucked away in the proverbial vaults for many years, available primarily to the stalwart researcher willing to make the trek to AFHRA in Montgomery, Alabama. To the average reader, the writing may seem dull or listless. Yet, their experiences will remain as fresh as a drive in a LaSalle or Jitterbugging to the Big Band sounds of Glenn Miller and Benny Goodman. This reprinting hopefully will bring new life to the people and events that helped shape the early years of Florida's primary military air field in the years leading up to World War II.

WILLIAM R. POLSON
6th Air Mobility Wing Historian
MacDill Air Force Base,
12 January, 2010

Sole source of printed material is used by permission from:
The Air Force Historical Research Agency (AFHRA)
Maxwell Air Force Base, Alabama

Permission of the photographs used within from:
Lynwood T (Grandson) and Jessica (Great Granddaughter) Jacobs
The Air Force Historical Research Agency (AFHRA)
MacDill Air Force Base History Office (Mr. Bill Polson)

Special Acknowledgements to:

Air Force Historical Research Agency (AFHRA), thank you for all the personnel I dealt with while I was doing my research and for their professionalism.

To the Maxwell Air Force Base billeting office, for providing a very comfortable stay while I was there doing my research.

And a special thank you to my wife Linda Lipowski, for her assistance and understanding, her typing skills, caring for our 3 children, for moving while doing this, for making this book go from a dream to a reality, well, for the whole military life style! Thank you, my dear, for your endurance.

BIRTH OF A BASE

MACDILL FIELD

1939-1941

TABLE OF CONTENTS

SUPPORTING DOCUMENTS

1. ABHq Barksdale Fld, La., Spec. Ord. #54, Extract, dated 7 Mar 1940.
2. ABHq MacDill Fld, Letr. To CG, 3rd AF, Subj: Administrative Reserve Officers, dated 7 Apr 41
3. ABHq Mitchell Fld, N. Y., Spec. Ord. #88, dated 15 Apr 40.
4. ABHq Barksdale Fld, La., Spec. Ord. #95, dated 27 Apr 40.
5. ABHq Langley Fld, Va., Spec. Ord. #114, Extract, dated 14 May 40.
6. Minutes of a Meeting Called to Organize a Post Exchange at MacDill Field, 5 June 1940.
7. Construction Program at the Air Corps Station MacDill Field, Fla., dated July 16-31, 1941.
8. 1st Ind. General Davis to Cg, MacDill Fld, File No. 413.56, dated 7 Dec 40.
9. Ltr. From Base Medical Inspector to The Surgeon, Station Hospital, MacDill Fld, Subj: Special Sanitary Report; Prophylactics Stations in the City of Tampa, dated 21 Dec 40.
10. Interview with Mr. C. P. Cannon.
11. Historical Data Supplied by Col. Lloyd Barnett.
12. Historical Summary of MacDill Field by Col. H. H. Young, A-1, 3rd AF.

ST. PETERSBURG
TAMPA BAY
TAMPA
ARMY AIRBASE
RESERVATION
HILLSBOROUGH BAY

C02-7771-21(R)(C)(1-8-40-11:05AJ)(12-1300) MACDILL FIELD, TAMPA, FLA.

CHAPTER I

SELECTION OF THE SITE

Increasing world tension caused by recurrent world political crises and sporadic armed clashes as well as the specter of great military power held by irresponsible authority caused the stirred American electorate to look to their defenses. Their previous parsimonious attitude toward the armed forces had left those defenses in a pitiable state. In a highly technological world, the American public had no other plan but to rely upon a levy of untrained troops to defend them, vaguely thinking that the equipment would somehow be furnished to carry on war. The impact of the reality of modern war as displayed by the undeclared wars in Spain, China, and Finland shattered the comfortable illusion and brought home to the American public the destructive power of war as technology had shaped it and forced the realization that long arduous training was necessary to prepare men and machines for war in the modern world.

Against the back drop of the impending tragedy in Europe that was destined to engulf our own country, and the awakening of the realization of our military weakness an aroused public opinion demanded effective air defenses from their political leaders. This demand was translated into action when new air bases were authorized to complement the handful that had been established by the Air Corps years before. One of these bases, it was announced, was to be located in Tampa. So it was that MacDill Field was born to the clashing accompaniment of wars and rumors of wars to come and it was to find its destiny in war.

It was on the 24th of May, 1939, that Major Lawrence L. Simpson received orders in the Tampa Office of the Constructing Quartermaster Corps of Engineers to proceed to the area known as Catfish Point for the purpose of taking immediate possession of that area for the purposes of the War Department. The order was signed by Secretary of War Woodring and it authorized the Constructing Quartermaster Engineers to proceed with the work of clearing the land and constructing the buildings necessary to develop the area into a modern air base when title to the land had been secured for the war Department. [1]

In compliance with these orders, Major Simpson had guards posted across the neck of land jutting out into Tampa Bay and announced that admittance to the area would be permitted only by passes issued by this office.

The area that the formal possession order brought under the control of the Quartermaster Corps, while the project awaited the final decision of the War Department concerning the location of the Southeastern Air Base, was composed of 5,767 acres. The area itself extended to the South of a line running from Ballast Point to the City of Port Tampa. The line turned to the South at the boundary line of Port Tampa for 3,000 feet where it turned Westward again and followed the boundary line to Old Tampa Bay.[2] After the area came under control of the War Department months were to elapse before the court procedures could be complied with and the property owners paid so that the work of construction could begin.

Although there was much to do before the property could be passed over to the actual ownership of the War Department, much had already been done before Secretary of War Woodring's order could be drawn up. In 1935, Congress had passed a Wilcox National Defense Act sponsored by Congressman Wilcox of Florida. This bill, though it provided seven additional air bases and depots, merely authorized the selection of bases and the Air Corps could have them constructed when it received the money to proceed.[3] In other words, the act was in the nature of a declaration of congressional policy and was probably indicative of awakening congressional interest in a more effective Air corps. Nevertheless, the Air Corps could only plan for the location of their sites as construction was out of the question until public opinion, aroused by the possibilities of impending military disaster, would permit Congress to authorize the needed funds.

While awaiting appropriations to implement the Wilcox national Defense Act, the Army Air Corps established a board of officers to pass upon the general location of the sites. The Wilcox Act provided that these seven bases should be established as follows: a base in Alaska; an air depot in the western United States; a base in the northeastern United States; a depot and a base in the southeastern United States; a base in Puerto Rico; and a base in Panama. To carry out the intent of this act, the Air Corps set up a board to pass on the selection of the actual sites. This board was known as the Wilcox Site Board and was composed of officers of the Air Corps and the War Department. The Air Corps Officers at the time that the air base was started were: Colonel John D. Reardon (now retired), Colonel Francis M. Brady (now General Brady), Major Rowland R. Street (now General Street), and Colonel Harry H. Young who later became Commanding Officer of MacDill Field. This board was charged with the selection of the site and, to a certain extent, was consulted on the plans for its construction.[4]

Since the Wilcox National Defense Act did not provide the funds for the new fields, it seems fair to consider it a statement of policy not only as an admission by Congress that the Air Corps should be enlarged but also a statement of the strategic policies accepted at the time. The list of seven localities was announced in Washington the 13th of July, 1939. The list provided for one base for the Territory of Alaska, located at Fairbanks. Far-western United States was given an Air Depot to be located at Ogden, Utah. New England received an air base that was not at the time announced but later located at Westover, Massachusetts. The Southeastern United States received two bases, one at Mobile, Alabama, an air depot, and another at Tampa, to be the Southeastern Air Base. The other two bases were to be established in Puerto Rico and Panama. The base in Panama was to be the second one for that area.

The official estimate of the expenditures for these bases was as follows:

The Alaskan Base to cost $4,000,000
The Ogden Air Depot to cost $8,000,000

The Northeastern Base to cost..$3,608,000
The Southeastern Base to cost..$8,000,000
The Mobile Air Depot to cost...$14,023,000
The Panama Air Base to cost...$6,799,000
(Tampa Tribune, 15 July 1939)

An analyses of the location of these sites and the estimated cost lead to the conclusion that the Caribbean Area was considered one of the most vulnerable points in the national defense. It is well to remember that the Caribbean Area is composed of small countries so lacking in military strength that a compact expeditionary force with modern equipment could seize them preliminary to a direct attack upon the United States. Likewise, the isolation of some of the islands would make it possible for enemy forces to establish secret air and submarine bases. From the vantage point of the Caribbean such establishments could make feasible attacks on the Panama Canal, shipping in the Gulf of Mexico, and the populous industrial cities of the Southeastern United States. Furthermore, such a foothold in these islands could be easily developed as a springboard for a full scale attack on the United States.

The possibilities of the success of such an attack would be increased by an air attack upon the Panama Canal. In fact, it was thought that a simple air raid from a carrier could have disastrous results for the Panama Canal[5]. Closing of the Canal would mean that it would be weeks before the Pacific Fleet could be joined to the much smaller Atlantic Fleet to aid in repelling an attack aimed at the heart of the industrial section of the United States.

In order to avoid the consequences of such eventualities, the Air Corps set up a triangular system of defense for the Caribbean. The apex of the triangle was to be in Puerto Rico and the two bases to be in Panama and Florida. Reliance was placed in patrols operating from this triangular system for early detection of an enemy attack and time to prepare effective counter offenses to repel it.

The Southeastern United States, as the continental base of the triangle, was assigned a dual role. It was to be an operational base from which heavy bombers were to operate in national defense, as well as a base of supplies to provide the men, airplanes and supplies necessary for the continuation of such operation for the whole Caribbean Area. [6] Operations were to be centered to the Southeastern Air Base at Tampa, Florida and logistics at the Air Depot at Mobile, Alabama.

The possible reasons given for the selection of Tampa are many, and none can be entirely authenticated. Certainly the Army investigated the weather record in the vicinity to determine the flying possibilities for the Weather Observer for Tampa and then reported to Washington that he had "supplied a considerable amount of climatological data of great value in determining the location of the site of Tampa."[7] This data probably revealed the fact that the Tampa vicinity had a record for flying weather that few sections of the nation could equal.[8]

In addition to fine flying weather the year around, Hillsborough County could offer a site to the Air Corps that had much to commend it. A narrow peninsula stretching for about two and one-half miles into the Tampa Bay, as measured from the City of Port Tampa, with an average width of two miles. This location could easily be separated from the adjoining land by fencing in one side of the area. In addition to this feature, the Base would be cooled by breezes blowing over the water on three sides, thereby benefiting the personnel.

More important, the site provided a maximum of safety for the flying field. The formation of the peninsula made it possible to locate the runways when completed so that six of the eight approaches were over water. This meant that no obstacles could be erected in the path of planes coming in for a landing. This advantage was obtained by virtue of the overwater approaches without having to go to the expense of acquiring land that would be useless to the purpose of the base, other than to eliminate obstructions being erected. Even so, the area was sufficiently large so that the two land approaches to the runways were located far enough from the boundaries of the base that no obstacles could possibly be built by civilian owners in the path of the planes.[9]

Finally, the proximity to Tampa was a vitally important consideration in fixing the location of the actual site. Here was a city that had a well developed transportation center for handling overland and water shipments, assuring a continuous flow of supplies for the proposed base and an easy method of transporting men. Furthermore, the railroad line that passed through the City of Port Tampa made it comparatively easy for a spur to be brought into the site. All this coupled with the fact that the City of Tampa itself could supply many of the needs for the base from the products of its own industry and skill, as well as help to house officers and non-commissioned officers, added to the attractiveness of the site in that vicinity.

The City of Tampa and County of Hillsborough were not behind handed in calling the natural advantages of the site to the attention of the Army Air Corps. Public enthusiasm was aroused by the Chamber of Commerce which established an Aeronautical Committee whose purpose was to keep the proposal uppermost in the minds of the City and County Officials and the business men of the vicinity. The committee also maintained a representative in Washington, Mr. Francis L. Judd, who devoted a great deal of his time to aiding Congressman J. Hardin Peterson in presenting the case for Hillsborough County and the City of Tampa to the War Department.

There can be little doubt but that the chamber of Commerce and the citizens of the city and county believed that they had an ideal location to offer and they were ready to make it even more attractive by buying three thousand acres of land to be used for the site and giving it to the War Department.[10] The State Legislature passed a Special Legislation to permit Hillsborough County to purchase three thousand acres of land to give to the War Department -- cost not to exceed $250,000.[11] The bill provided that money to pay for this grant could be raised by a levy of two mills on property in the general vicinity of Tampa if it was accepted by a referendum. Another bill provided that the land was to be donated to the War Department on a tax exempt basis. These bills provided the necessary legal basis for the County and City authorities to swing into action in acquiring the property although the referendum provision was not utilized since the County was able to sell bonds accepted for payment of taxes already levied to provide the necessary sums.[12]

The remainder of the property for the site amounting to 2,700 acres was to be provided by purchase by the War Department itself. In order to expedite the purchase, an effort was made to get property owners to agree to the terms generally agreed upon for the purchase of the property.

One of the greatest difficulties encountered was the large number of property holders owning land in the area and the difficulties in clearing the titles.[13] The owners of the property were warned by Mayor Chancey on his return from Washington with the news that the War Department was now ready to proceed with plans for the development of the site that the War Department had to get the land for a reasonable price and without difficulty. Failing this, it was possible that the site might be located elsewhere.[14]

In response to the appeals, some owners sold their land for one dollar an acre to the County.[15] The others were apparently glad to accept the general terms of fifty dollars an acre for the shore front property and ten dollars an acre for land lying inland. The principal difficulty encountered in the purchase of land was the tangle of taxes that seemed to have enmeshed the land. During the boom days of Florida when any kind of land sold for fabulous sums, a special tax district was created by referendum of the property holders of the area which established the Inter Bay Drainage District.[16] The district constructed ditches to drain the land to make it usable for a real estate subdivision, and the costs were charged against the property. With the terrific decline in property values that followed the boom, much land was allowed to revert to the state. Other property was maintained only to the extent necessary for the proprietors to maintain their property rights. In addition to these difficulties the Reconstruction Finance Corporation refinanced the District through a $1,100,000 loan and held a lien on the bonds issued by the Drainage District.[17] As a result of these complications, the property owners were unable to provide a clear title for the War Department without spending a great deal of money, probably more than they would receive.

In order to straighten out the muddled title situation, the War Department held conferences with Francis L. Judd, the Chamber of Commerce representative in Washington and Congressman J. Hardin Peterson to consider the situation. Among the conferees was Lt. Colonel R. D. Valliant, the Quartermaster Corps Real Estate Officer who was to be sent to Tampa to go over the title situation on the ground.[18]

It was recognized by the conferees that there were only two methods to settle the title problems. Either the reconstruction Finance Company would agree to lift the lien that it held on the property or condemnation proceedings would have to be used to get possession of the property. The proponents of the Tampa Bay site approached the R.F.C. with the argument that the value of the lien would be guaranteed by the increase in property values of the land outside the proposed site in the Bay to Bay area covered by the lien.[19] The alternative method of resorting to condemnation proceedings had made to commend itself to the authorities responsible for the construction of the Base. This method would permit the Army to take immediate possession of the property and commence the construction work, leaving the title problem to be cleared up by the courts.

At the beginning of the negotiations to clear the land titles, there seemed to have been some hope that direct dealings with the property owners would be successful. The County authorities continued to report progress in acquiring land in the latter part of July and the first of August.[20] Then it was suddenly announced that the Federal Government was going to take over the property by condemnation proceedings.[21] It is not clear just when this decision was made. It is very likely that the War Department had been prepared to take this step from the first and decided to await the results of the county authorities attempt to clear the land by direct negotiation. This decision may have been communicated to the County Commission when Lt. Colonel R. D. Valliant made his trip to Tampa to study the title problem. This was a closed meeting and its results were not announced to the press. A second meeting between Tampa representatives and the War Department was held in Washington to discuss the title situation on the 17th of August. Whatever course the negotiations may have taken, the announcements of the 27th of August represented the final decision.

When the Federal Government resorted to condemnation proceedings, the obligations of Hillsborough County was met by payment of a lump sum that was stipulated not to exceed $125,000 in lieu of the three thousand acres of land that had been promised. Land that was generally priced at $10.00 to $50.00 an acre.[22] The size of the check sent at the time of the announcement was not disclosed, but it was known at the time that it would not be for the full amount as there was a balance left that was to be paid "whenever required". When the order for the United States District Attorney to proceed with the suits was received it was finally announced that the County had paid $97,000 to which the War Department had added $76,004. The total of $173,004 was estimated by the War Department to be sufficient to pay off all legitimate claims against the property.[23]

Tampa was overjoyed at the announcement of the 15th of July, 1939 that the Southeastern Air Base was definitely going to be located at Catfish Point. The earlier announcement merely took possession of the area while it was under consideration. July 15th marked the final decision of the War Department.

To the people of Tampa, the coming of the Southeastern Air Base meant many things. It meant the increase of property values throughout the Tampa area. It meant business for the Tampa firms in supplying the needs of the Base and the personal needs of the men and officers to be stationed at such a post. Immediately, it meant employment for several thousand unemployed people in the work of constructing the base as well as providing future steady employment for the many civilians necessary to operate a military post. Indicative of the feelings of Tampa was a cartoon by George White in the Tampa Tribune for Saturday, July 15, 1939 depicting the Tampa skies full of planes dropping dollars on the city. It was a time of rejoicing for the citizens of Tampa.

BIBLIOGRAPHY

1. Tampa Tribune, 25 May 1939.
2. Tampa Tribune, 23 May 1939.
3. Historical data supplied by Colonel H. H. Young.
4. Interview with Colonel H. H. Young.
5. Tampa Tribune, Sunday, 10 December 1939, ph. II, p. 4, speech by Major General Delos C. Emmons.
6. Ibid.
7. Tampa Tribune, 15 July 1939, p. 7.
8. Weather data supplied by Lt. Leslie Heinen, Weather Forecaster, MacDill Field.
9. Based on an interview with Colonel W. V. Witcher, 4 February 1944, and an interview with Colonel H. H. Young on the same date.
10. Tampa Tribune, 15 July 1939.
11. Tampa Tribune, 23 May 1939.
12. Ibid.
13. Tampa Tribune, 15 July 1939, p. 7.
14. Tampa Tribune, 15 July 1939.
15. Tampa Tribune, 29 July 1939.
16. Interview with Mr. O. P. Cannon, Resident Engineer, MacDill Field, April 4, 1944.
17. Tampa Tribune, 25 July 1939.
18. Tampa Tribune, 17th, 19th, and 20th of July, 1939.
19. Tampa Tribune, 20 July 1939.
20. Tampa Tribune, 26th, 29th, and 8th of August, 1939.
21. Tampa Tribune, 27 August 1939.
22. Tampa Tribune, 27 August 1939.
23. Tampa Tribune, 30 September 1939.

—Photo by Roscoe Frey, Tribune Staff

ARMY OFFICERS CONFER ON AIR BASE
Lieut.-Col. L. B. Jacobs (left) and Maj. Lawrence L. Simpson

Colonel Lynwood B. Jacobs
Assumes command of Southeastern Air Base
8 Sept 1939

CHAPTER II

CONSTRUCTION: FIRST PHASE

Twelve days after the county passed over its check for the money to meet its obligations, Major Lawrence L. Simpson, Constructing Quartermaster, arrived in Tampa to supervise the preliminary steps in the construction of the field.

It was on the morning of the 6th of September, 1939 that the first crew to start actual work arrived on the site. The crew consisted of twenty-two engineers and their helpers who started the surveying of the area for the site.[1] Major Simpson's first headquarters was located on the fourth floor of the City Hall. These offices were to be the headquarters of the Constructing Quartermaster until the field was far enough along with its construction program to house the offices on the field. [2]

Two days later the first Southeastern Air Base Commander arrived in Tampa to look for a house. The commander was Lieutenant Colonel L. B. Jacobs, who had just been relieved as Chief of the Buildings and Grounds Section of The Office of the Chief of Air Corps[3]. The duties that Lt. Colonel Jacobs was to perform were essentially that of an aviation consultant to Major Simpson, the Constructing Quartermaster. While the duty of constructing the base was the responsibility of the Quartermaster Corps of Engineers, the problems of aviation were such that it was necessary to have someone with the specialized technical knowledge of those needs to represent the Air Corps. Therefore, Lt. Colonel Jacobs was sent to Tampa, with the invaluable experience as Chief of the Buildings and Grounds Section of the Office of the Chief of Air Corps to represent the Air Corps on the project. As he said of his duties with Simpson, "Together we'll map out the plans of construction and layout the base".[4] Such were to be his duties until the troops should arrive.

With the arrival of the responsible officers and their assisting crews and office force, the preliminary steps were taken to convert the 5,700 acres of Florida waste land into a modern air base. Major Simpson's first act was to start a crew of twenty-two men on the job of surveying the land. The very morning that the Major and his men arrived, the 5th of September, 1939, saw the crew at work. The first job that was undertaken was the measurement of the area that the War Department was to receive. The work began from the beach mark that had been established by the Harbor Survey of the United States District Engineers of Jacksonville, Florida at the extreme end of the peninsula known as Manhattan Beach.[5]

From this point the surveying crews ran their lines to establish the boundary lines and to measure the exact size of the area. Likewise, this was the starting point for the work in making up the contour map of the area. While this surveying work was going on, undertaken to provide data for the construction of the field, other data were being gathered by soil drilling tests to determine the depth of the stratum of bed rock and sampling the soil by digging hundreds of holes 4 feet by 6 feet.

With this data, Lt. Colonel Jacobs and Major Simpson began the work of drawing up the plans for the base. By the 3rd of November the plans had progressed to the point where a conference could be held to explain and consider objections raised by members of the Office of Chief of Air Corps and the Quartermaster General in Washington, who arrived in Tampa on the 4th of November.[6] The members of the conference representing the Office of the Chief of Air Corps were Lieutenant Colonel Otto G. Trunk, Chief of the Buildings and Grounds Section, Major W. G. Smith of the Radio and Communications Section, and Lieutenant Colonel Harry H. Young, Chief of the Reserve Section. The member of the conference representing the Quartermaster General's Office was Major Howard B. Nurse.

According to the original recommendations, the building program would have been projected along the Northern boundary, starting from the old Bayshore Road on the East and running to the West. This would have brought the barracks and administration buildings up to the main gates and visitors would have come in directly to the cantonment area. The buildings then would have been placed on the highest ground in the area and the necessity for fill would have been avoided to a great extent. Furthermore, the area was sufficiently large and so arranged that future expansion would have been provided that would have utilized the field to its fullest extent. The runways and hangars were, under this plan, to be located to the South and East of the proposed building area. Under this plan, the runways would have been provided with 6 overwater approaches, which meant that no obstructions to the field could ever be erected.[7]

Although the plan was soundly conceived to utilize the possibilities of the field for an air base to the utmost for the least cost and had the support of all the engineers on the ground, it was rejected in Washington. No doubt the merits of the proposed plan were recognized in Washington, but other council prevailed with the result that the final plan placed the building to the Southeast of the locations selected in the first plan. This necessitated that the hangars and runways be changed from their original location. The hangars were transferred to the Western end of the building area where they formed a semi-circle running to the Southeast and Northwest, dominating the great runways. The runways themselves were shifted to the Northwest of the location originally planned for them so that they are now the first sight that the visitor beholds on entering the gates of the Field.

The area selected for the building site, the lowest part of the Field, was made up of ponds and swamp-land that had to be eliminated before it was possible to erect buildings. To accomplish this, it was necessary to raise the level of the entire building area from two to four feet throughout, a large additional expense which could have been avoided if the original plan had been accepted. The virtue of the second plan was that it put the living quarters closer to the water front where it had the advantage of cooling breezes from the Bay during the long season of hot weather. The new plan retained the feature of 6 overwater approaches from the previous plan. In addition to this, enough space was provided for the installation of other runways, although the approaches had to be overland.[8]

On the 20th of November, a general outline of the plan for the field, as revised in Washington, was received by Major Simpson, and the actual work of clearing the site, in accordance with that plan, could be started.[9] Meanwhile, the construction of the base was greatly facilitated by the appropriation of $1,064,255 from the WPA Funds.[10] This source for additional money to build the base was indicated from the very inception of the project when it was indicated that the WPA would most likely aid in the construction of the continental bases by the employment of those on its rolls.[11] The tentative allotments for the Southeastern Air Base were announced by the Secretary of War -- Woodring, when he allocated $2,835,000 of the Army Defense and $876,200 of WPA funds on July 21st.[12] One of the first statements that Major Simpson made on his arrival in Tampa was to the effect that he and State Administrator Roy Schroeder, were already at work on plans to utilize WPA labor.[13] Thus the announcement on the 10th of November, that President Roosevelt had approved the plan filed in Washington by the Florida WPA Administration, Mr. Roy Schroeder[14], occasioned little surprise.

A breakdown of the funds allotted to the project by the WPA, as made by Congressman J. Hardin Peterson, provided that WPA Funds would be expended in providing labor for the clearing and grading of the site, installing drainage, roads, fencing, railroad tracks, water and sewage systems, electrical and telephone facilities and constructing buildings and runways. For this work, WPA allotted $517,745 for labor and $59,136 for equipment and supplies. Supplementing the WPA Funds for the work done by the labor they provided the War Department contributed $450,064 for equipment, materials and supplies and $4,450 for labor.

With the funds allocated and work planned, Mr. Rex Wilson and Mr. O. P. Cannon were sent to the site with a small group of workmen, to prepare temporary headquarters for the WPA from which the work of clearing the site, in accordance with the final plans, was to be administered. There Mr. Wilson and Mr. Cannon were to confer and plan the work to be done with Mr. Louis E. Ebling, Civilian Construction Superintendent of the Quartermaster Corps. Then on the 27th of November 1939, a crew of one hundred men went to work on the job. Before the advent of the one hundred crew, news arrived that the WPA quota for the Tampa Area had been increased to provide for 2000 jobs on the Southeastern Air Base by Colonel Farrington, the National Director of WPA.[15] With this number which provided for eventual employment on the Base, the work could be speeded along so that the first detachment of enlisted personnel which was expected to arrive in the Spring about the first of April, could be housed properly.[16]

It must have been a depressing sight that greeted the crew of one hundred men who went to work on Monday morning, the 27th of November. It must have seemed almost impossible to their untrained eyes to convert the wilderness that made up the area that was to be the Southeastern Air Base. It was made up of typical Florida waste land consisting of palmettos, mangroves, scrub pine, oak trees, ponds and swamps. But it must have been of some pride to them that they were part of a great project, upon whose completion was pinned the hopes of Tampa for a prosperous future, and the hopes of the Air Corps and the National Defense Program for a strong and capable installation for the defense of the country.

There was plenty of evidence that the people of Tampa were taking a vital interest in the job that the workmen were starting. Although the formal opening ceremony that had been planned was abandoned because certain members of the state and national dignitaries could not attend, newspaper photographers were busy snapping the pictures of the men working on the job of cleaning out the old drainage ditches, pulling out the palmettos and felling the trees that clustered around the entranceway at the end of Lisbon Avenue.

This work that was being undertaken on that sunny morning on the 28th of November was very shortly to become something very much more personalized than a Southeastern Air Base, a general name used by the Wilcox National Defense Act when it was passed in 1935. Now it was to receive its own name. On the first of December word arrived in Tampa that the field was henceforth to be known as MacDill Field. The name was selected in the honor of Colonel Leslie MacDill who had died as the pilot of an Air Corps plane on November 8th, 1938 at Anacostia, D.C. The Colonel had spent almost his entire army career, which began in 1912, in Army Aviation. His death was the result of engine trouble that developed just as he was taking off from Bolling Field. As a result of his service, his name was selected to be the new designation for the Southeastern Air Base.

Meantime, the plans were being completed in Washington and on the 5th of December Major General Henry H. Arnold arrived in Tampa with them. From that time on work could proceed according to fixed plans.

The first jobs to be done for constructing the field were to open the drainage ditches and construct temporary roads to transport the necessary machinery and supplies to the building area. In constructing the ditches, it was fortunate for the program that embraced the first phase of construction that there was already a drainage system in existence. That system was inherited form the old Inter Bay Drainage District that had caused and was causing so much trouble in unraveling the titles to the site. Now the drainage ditches of the District was working for the benefit of the field. The system provided by these main ditches and their subsidiaries provided a network that covered the area. The only thing necessary to do to complete the drainage was to clear the ditches, one of the first jobs tackled by the WPA and one that was to continue until the field was completed and the ditches walled up with concrete[17].

The next step taken in the development of the field was the construction of temporary roads to transport the needed machinery, equipment, and supplies to the building area. The building area being taken to include the runway and hangar section and the site of the first permanent barracks.

Fortunately for the road building program, there was a fairly serviceable road that had been constructed for the use of the Public Health Service in getting to the Quarantine Station at the southern end of the peninsula. This road, known as the Bayshore Road, skirted by the bay from the entrance to the field to the Station. Being paved with brick, it was serviceable enough for the work to be required of it during the construction of the first building program, though it had been abandoned later.

Colonel Leslie MacDill

On November 30, 1938, the Secretary of War announced that the new Army Air Base to be built in Tampa would be named after Col Leslie MacDill, and aviator who had been killed when his combat training plane crashed in Washington D.C. three weeks earlier. MacDill, at the age of 29, had been the commander after World War I of an aviation training school in France that used mostly Sopwith Camels. MacDill was also one of the first Americans to be awarded a doctorate in aeronautical engineering from the Massachusetts Institute of Technology

The first road to be started was one that ran from Lisbon Avenue, now MacDill Avenue, in a direction that was almost due south, along the route of the present MacDill Avenue, where MacDill Avenue now stops at the flying field. This temporary road turned to the east, skirting the northeastern end of the present Northeast-Southwest runway. A few yards past the location of the runway, the road turned again toward the east and continued to the present site of hangar Number 5. There it took a more southerly direction and stretched out to the site of the present Post Exchange Building.

The second road to be completed was one that ran from the "borrow pit" that had been developed to supply fill for construction purposes. This area was in the northwestern section of the field, and the road, starting at that point, ran in a southeasterly direction to join the first road at a point about 1,500 feet from the Lisbon, or MacDill Avenue Gate. Still another road was constructed that ran along the north boundary to the "borrow pit". This provided quick, easy access to the pit from Lisbon or MacDill Avenue, as well as the administrative offices and shops. The other road providing for the carriage of the fill to the building area.

In the building area itself, a road was built that was actually a projection of the one that ran from the MacDill Avenue Gate to the site of the Post Exchange. This road connected that site with the Bayshore Road, running in back of the Benjamin House and in front of the present site of the Officers' Club to the Bayshore Road. Later this road was developed to be the present Florida Avenue.

Completing the system of roads was one that was built along the north boundary of the site connecting the entrances to the field at MacDill Avenue and at Bayshore Drive. Thus the systems of temporary roads were developed as a circulatory network that gave access to every part of the field from the two principle roads coming from Tampa.[18]

While the work on the roads was being carried forward, other WPA crews were engaged in clearing the field. This work began on the site for the runways and was extended to the area where the barracks were to be built later on. This work consisted of cutting down the trees which were trimmed and hauled away to be used for lumber, and cutting out the brush which was burned on the ground. After the ground cover had been removed, heavy discs were used to tear up the soil and destroy the roots. The logs, to which the trees had been reduced, were taken to the little saw mill that had been set up near the MacDill Avenue gate. There they were cut into lumber to be used for temporary buildings and sheathing in constructing the sewers and underground conduits for utilities to be used on the base. It is worthy of note that the little saw mill cut more than one million feet of lumber from the trees that had to be removed from the area that was cleared on the site.

The conditions that faced the men who were doing the preliminary work are almost unbelievable to men who live on MacDill Field today. Mosquitoes arose in swarms to meet the men when they came to work and were still busily attacking them when they left. The workers had to wear high boots, or wrap their legs with burlap sacking in order to protect themselves against the greatest danger, if not the greatest annoyance - snakes. Great, big, fat diamond-back rattle-snakes were over 6 feet long and ready to dispute the right of way with the men engaged in surveying, clearing, or building the roads. These were killed, literally, by the thousands before the work was completed. Despite the fact that the snakes outnumbered the human population on the site, and the number of civilians employed went over 5000 at one time, there was not a single case of snake-bite reported to the authorities[19].

By the end of 1939 much of the work had been accomplished for MacDill Field even though the Field itself retained much of the untamed aspect that it had when the Army took possession on the 24th of May of that year. The best description of the appearance of the field has been provided by Colonel Lloyd Barnett, who first saw the site about Christmas of 1939.

"I got my first view of what was to be MacDill Field in the month of December, at which time I was on leave of absence in Florida. Having known and served with Major Leslie MacDill in 1918 in France, and hoping to be transferred to MacDill Field for duty, I was keenly interested in the establishment of this, the first of the group of new bases to be set up in the long delayed expansion of the Air Corps. The approach to the site of the new base was via what is now MacDill Avenue - then a narrow sand road. My car got stuck in the deep sand and the last three hundred yards leading up to MacDill Avenue Gate was negotiated by man-power. That is, a group of WPA workers pushed my car the last part of the trip.

"From the gate one could see only a vast sweep of scrub pine trees, palmetto growth, and (towards the bay front) low swampy ground. The trees had been felled along the proposed runways, and through the trees toward the water front could be seen the clearing operations taking place in the sandy swamps. To the layman this would have appeared an impossible site for the development of an Air Base. But, having pioneered in early 1917 in the settling and building of Camp Kelly (now Kelly Field) Texas, I was not dismayed at the prospects facing those pioneers of MacDill Field."

(024-777I-2IR)(6-14-40-3:47P)(12-1500) BUILDING AREA &
MACDILL FIELD FLA.

(058-777I-21R)(9-10-40-11:35A)(12-300) HOSPITAL, MACDILL FIELD FLA

RESTRICTED
(064-777-21R)(10-1-40-9:30A)(12-2000)(MACDILL FIELD, TAMPA, FLA
RESTRICTED

RESTRICTED
(0102·777I·21RX12·2·40-1:06P)(12·350)
MACDILL FIELD, FLA.

BARRACKS AREA, MACDILL FIELD, FLA.
SECRET

REFERENCES

1. Tampa Tribune, 6 September 1939.
2. Tampa Tribune, 8 September 1939.
3. S. O. #199, WD, Washington, D. C., 26 August 1939.
4. Tampa Tribune, 8 September 1939.
5. Tampa Tribune, 6 September 1939.
6. Tampa Tribune, 3rd and 5th of November 1939; Tampa News, 6 November 1939.
7. Based on an interview with Mr. O. P. Cannon, Resident Engineer, MacDill Field.
8. The foregoing is based on an interview with Mr. O. P. Cannon, Resident Engineer, MacDill Field.
9. Tampa Times, 20 November 1939.
10. Tampa Tribune, 10 November 1939.
11. Tampa Tribune, 15 July 1939, p. 7.
12. Tampa Tribune, 22 July.
13. Tampa Tribune, 6 September 1939.
14. Tampa Tribune, 24 October 1939.
15. Tampa Tribune, 23 November 1939.
16. Tampa Times, 8 September 1939.
17. Interview with Mr. O. P. Cannon, Resident Engineer, and Tampa Tribune, 29 November 1939.
18. Material for description of temporary road building based on interview with Mr. O. P. Cannon, Resident Engineer.
19. Based on an interview with Mr. O. P. Cannon, Resident Engineer, MacDill Field.

CHAPTER III

PLANS FOR THE SITE

When the surveying and mapping was completed, and the clearing and temporary road building work started, preliminary work could begin on the construction of the buildings. The final draft of the plans for the location and type of building was brought to Tampa by Major General H. H. Arnold on the 5th of December, 1939. At that time, General Arnold went over the plans with Colonel Lynwood B. Jacobs, Commanding Officer of the field and Major Lawrence L. Simpson, the Constructing Quartermaster. Upon receipt of the plans and instructions, the Constructing Quartermaster Corps was ready to start the building program.

The size of the trust was fixed by the final plans at 5,767 acres. This is the site of the field as it is today, for the land was the outright property of the War Department and additional land has not been leased.

The buildings to be erected called for both permanent and temporary buildings. Some installations, such as the hangars and warehouses, were to be permanent, but the barracks and administration buildings were to be temporary. When negotiations for the Field were still going on it was announced by the Air Corps and the War Department that MacDill Field was to be a permanent installation with permanent buildings. The style of the buildings, it was said, was to be of the Spanish or Mediterranean type in order to provide as much comfort as possible for the personnel during the long hot Florida summers.[1] But the plan that General Arnold brought to Tampa must have included temporary buildings for the enlisted men's living quarters, for on the 12th of December, 1939, Major Simpson announced the construction of 31 buildings of that type.[2] It was very likely the intention of the Air Corps and the War Department to construct permanent buildings but the rapidity with which the Air Corps was expanded during 1940 produced a situation that forced the authorities to change their plans. Nevertheless, several units of the permanent type were constructed, but it was the temporary type of building that was to dominate the architectural style of the field outside the "Vital Area" or Hangar and Warehouse Section.

General Arnold brought plans with him to Tampa on the 6th of December, 1939 that were drawn up for a military installation with a strength of 1,600 officers and men. [3] It was in accordance with these plans for the military strength of the field that the first building program was started. The only one of the several buildings on the site that could be utilized was the Benjamin House. This structure of stucco that had been the home of the Benjamin family, was set aside to become the Officers' Club. The new buildings that were to be constructed included:

Two hangars and a Shop estimated to cost approximately $1,200,000[4]; four warehouses estimated at $200,000[5]; a photographic laboratory to cost $35,000[6]; and a communications building that would include the guard house and fire house estimated to cost $50 - 60,000 dollars.[7] The total expenditure of Air Corps funds to be $1,785,000.

In addition to these permanent buildings, the plan to erect the temporary quarters for the enlisted men was announced.[8] This group of buildings were to include 17 barracks of the double-decker type to house 63 men each, 8 mess halls capable of feeding 250 men each, and 6 day rooms which were to be used not only for recreation rooms but supply rooms as well. These were the first buildings to be started because they were necessary to house the first shipment of troops that were scheduled to arrive at the field around the 15th of April. In order to rush the work so as to complete it in time, it was decided to use WPA labor and put them to work using the rough lumber that could be quickly provided, rather than wait on the slow process of letting contracts for the work.[9] At first, it was thought that contracts would be let to install the necessary utilities, plumbing and heating, and to roof the structures. But later on it was found necessary to complete the whole project with the WPA labor.

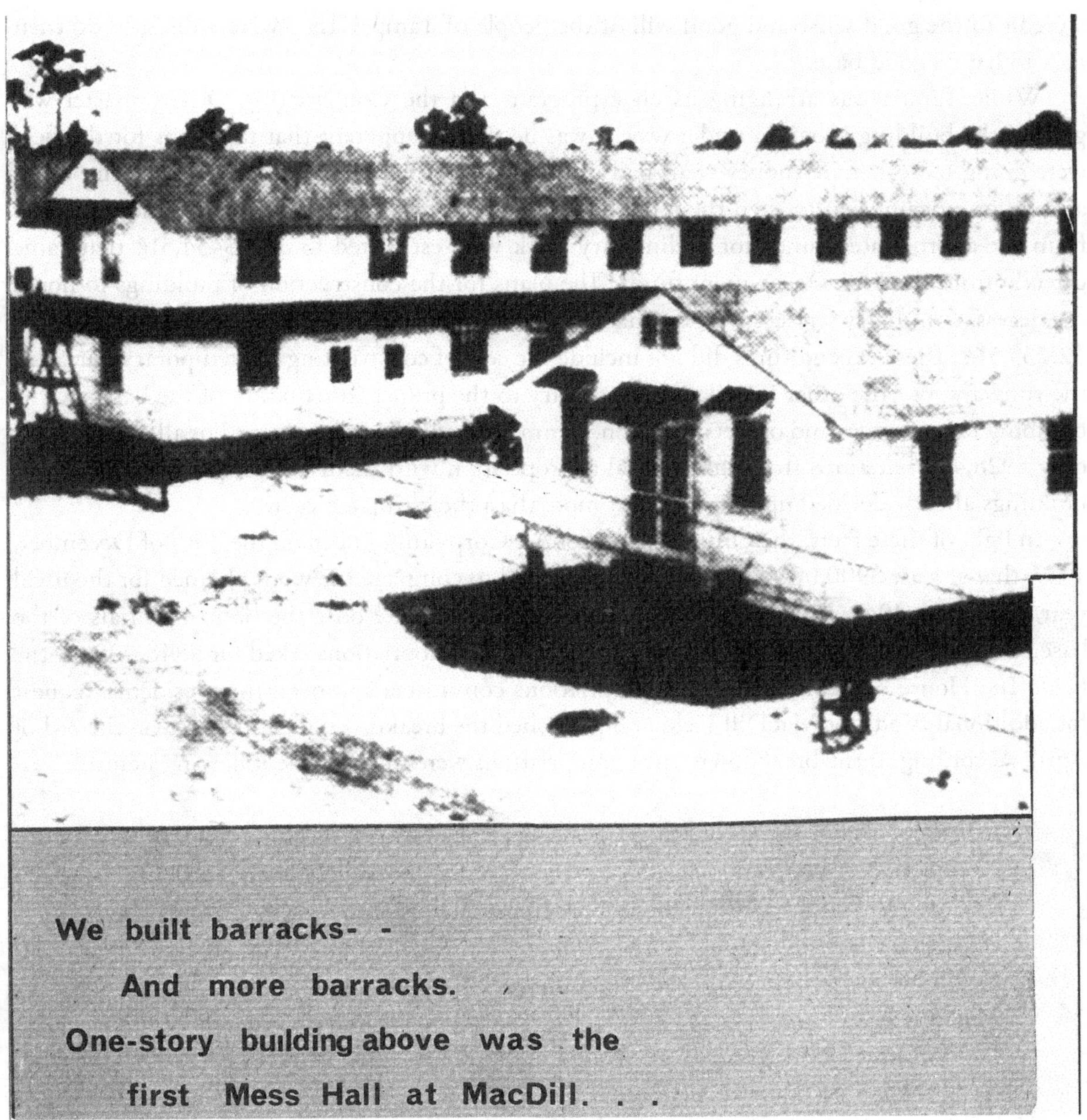

We built barracks- -
And more barracks.
One-story building above was the first Mess Hall at MacDill. . .

In providing for the myriad details necessary for the proper functioning of the field as planned, the City of Tampa played a most effective part. The city agreed to provide the water for the Base from its own reservoirs. To implement this plan the city asked for bids for 6,000 feet of 12 inch pipe on the 12th of December, 1939. In addition to this, the citizens of Tampa, through the Chamber of Commerce, sponsored a program to procure housing and a downtown club house for enlisted men. The housing program was to list 300 housing units that could be leased to military personnel for as low a rental as possible. The club house that was sponsored was to be a combination club and waiting room located at the bus terminal planned to run to the field when it got in operation. The club was to furnish a lounge for letter writing and reading and a certain amount of recreation. Vital services to provide for the smooth operation of the base and a credit to the good sense and good will of the people of Tampa. They were willing to do their part to have a good base.

While Tampa was arranging its civic program and the Constructing Quartermaster was getting the building program under way, it was becoming apparent that the plans for the field were going to cost more money than had originally been planned and allocated for the work, a situation not unusual to even the most humble builder of his own home. The amounts spent from the appropriated funds for preliminary work were estimated to cost $454,514 that came directly from the War Department funds. The plans for the construction of buildings to house the necessary military services were estimated to increase the bill $1,785,000, to bring the total to $2,239,514. These expenditures did not include the cost of constructing the temporary barracks, the runways, nor the other installations necessary to the proper functioning of the base such as bombing target ranges and officers' and non-commissioned officers' quarters. For all of this work, only $928,486 remained from the original appropriation with the usual danger that even those buildings already decided upon might cost more than the estimated cost.

In light of these facts, the Office of Chief of Air Corps announced on the 30th of December, 1939, that at least $900,000 more would be required to complete the work planned for the fiscal year, ending in 1941. This money was to be used to complete only the basic essentials of the base. The presidential budget message for the 1940-41 appropriations asked for $848,000 for the field. The House of Representatives appropriations committee approved the president's request for additional funds for MacDill Field and published the breakdown of the figures on the 3rd of April. According to the breakdown, the appropriations were to cover the following items:

Runways, Grading and Lighting	$400,000
Completion of Hangars	$183,400
Addition to Gasoline Storage	$50,000
Headquarters Building	$131,000
Bomb Storage	$50,000
Machine Gun Range	$15,000
Water, Electricity, Etc.	$18,500

With this promised reinforcement for the War Department funds, additional money to the amount of $289,000 was provided from WPA sources. According to Senator Andrews, these funds were provided directly from WPA funds and War Department funds that were derived from the general appropriations from Congress and allocated to the Army for construction purposes. This brought WPA Expenditures to $1,353,302 exclusive of direct congressional appropriations of WPA funds for the field of $1,800,000 or a total of $3,153,302 supplied from funds other than the formal War Department funds.

While the funds to construct the field were in the process of being brought together, conferences were being held to expedite the building program in getting such matters as plans and contracts settled as rapidly as possible. The process of getting the contracts depended upon getting the plans finally approved. Then the plans and specifications had to be sent to prospective bidders at their request after the announcement had been made that the proposed work was open for bidding. By its very nature, the process was slow. In the case of MacDill Field it seemed agonizingly slow in the opening stages of the building program.

The principal difficulty seemed to be the tardiness with which the final plans and specifications were received. On the 26th of January, 1940, a committee from Washington arrived in Tampa to confer on these matters. This committee was composed of Brigadier General R. C. Moore of the General Staff, Colonel E. B. Gregory, Acting Quartermaster General, Major H. B. Nurse of the Planning Branch of the Quartermaster General's Office, and L. C. Rosenburg, Consulting Architect to the Quartermaster General.

The make-up of this committee stamps it as primarily one interested in planning details, and this is borne out by the statement of Colonel Gregory after rendering the usual happy felicitations to the people of Tampa on the importance of MacDill Field in comparison to all others. "There is a lot of engineering and planning to do on the hangars and shop", said the Colonel, warning the public that the work on the hangars and shops would take 8 or 10 months to complete.

But it wasn't only the hangars and shops that presented difficulties in getting the final plans completed. Brigadier General (now Major General) Barton K. Yount in his inspection of the base in the latter part of February found many things that were hardly as complicated as the hangars that were without plans. There were no plans made by the latter part of February for the sewerage and electric system. Warehouses and officer quarters were also provided for on the field plans and in the appropriation list, but no details of the plans nor specifications had been received[11].

This state of affairs angered General Yount and he bluntly called the situation "absurd". He pointed out that those responsible for the planning of the Field had had the money for these installations since July of 1939 and hadn't produced a plan to that date. To understand the source of his irritation it is necessary to realize that the plans were already drawn up to bring troops to the Field in the latter part of April[12], and not even a plan for such essential services as sewerage and electricity had been planned. General Yount felt that the only way to get the desired action would be to have "Brett (Brigadier General Brett, Assistant Chief of the Air Corps) himself get after it".

The tenor of General Yount's letter seemed to point an accusing finger to the Constructing Quartermaster Corps as being responsible for the delay in getting the plans to Major Simpson, himself an officer in that Corps, so that the bids could be let. It was the Quartermaster Corps that had the authority over and responsibility for the planning and construction of the Field. Of course the plans were supervised by the Office of the Chief of the Air Corps, but only to see that their technical needs would be fulfilled by the plans submitted. That is, the Air Corps had the authority to see to it that the arrangement of the Field adequately utilized the location so that it would be useable for the taking off and landing of planes; that the hangars made good use of the money allotted to them for that purpose; that the buildings, in general, were convenient to the work in hand. Thus the plans were the responsibility of the Quartermaster Corps.

When the plans were held up so that contracts could not be let, or, if WPA labor was to be used, supplies could not be obtained until the organizations were ready to move on to the Field, the Air Corps could do little about it. Certainly little could be done from MacDill Field.

In fact, General Yount's estimate of the situation was that Colonel Jacobs and the Constructing Quartermaster were getting along very well and he did not "think that the trouble lies down here". For that reason it required, he said, "someone in authority to go to the powers that be" to get the job done.[13]

There were some bright spots in the rather gloomy picture presented by General Yount. Among them was the work on the water situation. General Yount reported that the City of Tampa was doing its part to get the water to the Field in time for its opening and the Constructing Quartermaster had ordered the pipes to install the system for the field. Likewise, the railroad spur coming from the City of Port Tampa was progressing well with a big crew of WPA workmen clearing the right of way.[14]

BIBLIOGRAPHY

1. Tampa Tribune, 6 December 1939.
2. Tampa Tribune, 12 December 1939.
3. Tampa Tribune, 12 December 1939.
4. Tampa Tribune, 10 December 1939.
5. Tampa Tribune, 26 March 1940.
6. Tampa Tribune, 19 December 1939.
7. Tampa Tribune, 3 March 1940.
8. Tampa Tribune, 12 December 1939.
9. Tampa Tribune, 12 December 1939.
10. Tampa Tribune, 30 December 1939.
11. Letter from General Young to Major General H. H. Arnold, 21 February, 1940.
12. Tampa Tribune, 12 December 1939.
13. Letter from Brigadier General Barton K. Yount to Major General H. H. Young, 21 February 1940, paragraph 8.
14. Ibid.

Lieutenant Colonel Harry H. Young
Assumes command of MacDill Field
18 March 1940

CHAPTER IV

COLONEL YOUNG'S ADMINISTRATION

It was on this rather discordant note of conflict between the authorities responsible for the construction of the Field that Lieutenant Colonel Harry H. Young came to MacDill for a tour of duty that was destined to last for two years. During that time Colonel Young was to see this Field grow to almost its fullest extent and start to play its part in the prosecution of the war that seemed far away in Europe when he came to Tampa. This first assignment of Colonel Young to MacDill Field required that he temporarily act as the Commanding Officer of the Field in place of Colonel Jacobs. Colonel Jacobs in his turn was relieved of duty as the Commanding Officer of the Field without troops and assigned as Technical Advisor to the Constructing Quartermaster.

This arrangement permitted Colonel Jacobs to continue with the task that he had already been engaged upon without having to worry about the impending arrival of organizations that were to take over the Field. This was to be the duty of Colonel Young. The assignment of Colonel Young to the Field was announced in Washington the 26th of February.[1] According to his orders, Colonel Young was given a leave which did not require him to report to the Field until the 18th of March, 1940.[2] The leave period was employed by Colonel and Mrs. Young to find a home to live in, arriving in Tampa on the 1st of March for the purpose.[3]

The new Commanding Officer had had a long and distinguished career in the Army before reporting to MacDill Field. He had entered the Army from the New Jersey National Guard, where he had been Sergeant Major in the Headquarters Company of the 4th Infantry. He was commissioned a second lieutenant in that organization on the 30th of December, 1916, and was promoted to first lieutenant on the 13th of April, 1917. On the 5th of August, 1917, Colonel Young transferred to the Aviation Section of the Signal Corps. On the 13th of September, 1920, he was accepted as a first lieutenant in the Air Service. Thereafter, Colonel Young rose in rank until he was appointed Lieutenant Colonel with temporary status on the 16th of June, 1939, the commission that he held when he came to MacDill Field.[4] Colonel Young had seen service in France with the 8th U.S. Observation Squadron. On returning to the United States he was placed in charge of organizing the 4th Observation Squadron which he took to Hawaii. After completing his tour of duty in Hawaii he was sent to Kelly Field, San Antonio, Texas for more training. In 1931 he graduated from the Tactical School, and the Command and General Staff School at Fort Leavenworth, Kansas, in 1936. In addition to his Army training, Colonel Young had been assigned to duty with the Air Corps Board at Langley Field for two years and had served with the National Guard in Missouri for four years. In addition to this service he had been on duty in the Office of the Chief of Air Corps for four years and it was from that duty that he was transferred to MacDill field.[5]

The arrival of Colonel Young was not the first contact that he had had with MacDill Field. As a member of the Army Wilcox Board which authorized the selection of the site he had been connected with the developments of the Field from the time that it was only an idea.[6] He had visited the Field to confer about the plans with others of the Air Corps and Quartermaster Corps on the 4th of November 1939.[7] Likewise, having been serving in the Office of the Chief of the Air Corps he had been appraised of the arrangements to activate the base. So the new Commanding Officer was thoroughly grounded in the facts concerning the Field and was not approaching a problem unknown to him.

Colonel Young's assignment was strictly a temporary one to make the necessary preliminary arrangements before the arrival of the tactical groups to be stationed on the Field. His successor had already been decided upon before the Colonel had left Washington at least. His successor was to be Colonel Clarence L. Tinker, than a Group Commander at Barksdale Field. In fact, it was Brigadier General Yount's opinion that Colonel Tinker should arrive on the field about the middle of March, or the time that Colonel Young arrived. The fact that Colonel Tinker had contributed the information would indicate that he was anxious to get to the Field to make his own arrangements to receive the military personnel. [8] Whatever the reasons, General Arnold did not authorize the change in plans as proved by later events.

The duties that Colonel Young was to discharge were those concerned with making the necessary arrangements for a field capable of training bombing crews for the Air Corps. This duty he approached with considerable enthusiasm as evidenced by a letter written a year later to a friend. "I have said time and time again that this station (MacDill Field) will eventually be the biggest, the best, and the safest airport in the country, because we are on a peninsula of good size and six out of our eight runways are from the water, without obstructions of any kind."[9]

One of Colonel Young's first duties was to arrange for a staff capable of carrying on the administration of a field devoted to the problem of training bombing crews. It was necessary that several officers that were to occupy key positions on this field should be brought to the field in plenty of time to make the arrangements that would enable them to discharge their duties when the field was opened. General Yount had suggested that a Post Quartermaster, a Medical and a Supply Officer would be sent down in advance of the arrival of the first detachment. In carrying out these duties, Colonel Young's first special order after assuming command was to designate Lieutenant Colonel Lynwood B. Jacobs as Executive Officer. [10] The experience that Colonel Jacobs had had as Commanding Officer and Air Corps Advisor to the Constructing Quartermaster on the field was especially valuable in this new position. He was acquainted with all the details concerning the field as well as the many arrangements for its construction that had been made between the Office of the Chief of Air corps and the Quartermaster General's Offices in Washington. In addition to these qualifications, the length of Colonel Jacob's stay in Tampa had enabled him to make valuable contacts with the official circles in Tampa so that the many details necessary to be worried out between the City and the authorities of the Field could be more easily arranged.

The second appointment made to staff the officer personnel of the Field was that which brought Major Lloyd Barnett to the Field on the 29th of March 1940, from duty at Langley Field.[11] Major Barnett was to be the Air Corps Supply Officer for the Field. Major Barnett was an Air Corps Officer with a great deal of experience in aeronautical affairs as well as services in the Air Corps from its inception. A pioneer in aviation (he had taken up flying as a civilian in 1912) he had enlisted in the Air Service of the Signal Corps in April 1917. After his enlistment he was shipped to Texas where he was a member of one of the first organizations to be stationed at Camp Kelly, later Kelly Field. Thus Major Barnett's first introduction to the Air Corps had to do with "pioneering" air fields, now he was called upon to do it again. He was assigned to a flight training school in Tours, France where he received his commission as a 2nd Lieutenant on the 18th of May, 1918. On the first of July 1920, he was given a Regular Army 2nd Lieutenant's commission in the Air Corps. Thereafter, he rose in the ranks of commissioned officers until he received his majority in October of 1939. Meanwhile, his flying experience was such that he was automatically granted the advanced ratings for pilots and technical observers when those ratings were established by the Air Corps. As a result, Major Barnett was rated as Command Pilot, Combat Observer, Aircraft Observer, and Technical Observer when he reported to MacDill Field.

The broad experience of Major Barnett in aviation was supplemented by considerable administrative experience. He was in command at Lawson Field, Ft. Banning, Georgia from 1931 to 1936. He commanded the 28th Bombardment Squadron at Nichols Field in Manila and later commanded Clark Field, Fort Statsenburg, North of Manila during his tour of duty in the Philippine Islands from 1936 to 1938. While at Clark Field, Major Barnett had the experience of being sent to Japan to make an inspection tour of aviation activities there and an economic survey. Thus Major Barnett came to the new field with a broad background of training and experience in both aviation and military administration.

Another step in bringing the key personnel to the field when it was announced the first of March, 1940, that Major Louis C. Dill was being sent to MacDill Field to be the Base Quartermaster. Major Dill was being transferred from the Sixth Division at Camp Jackson, Columbia, South Carolina. Major Dill had also had a long career in the Army, entering the service through the Louisiana National Guard where he had enlisted and served through the enlisted grades in Company F of the First Infantry. He was commissioned a 2nd Lieutenant in the Regular Army. From that time forward, Major Dill rose in the commissioned ranks of the Infantry until he was commissioned a Major the first of August, 1935. Then on the 15th of June 1937 he transferred to the Quartermaster Corps. [12]

The appointment of Major Dill to Colonel Young's staff brought him to MacDill Field as Base Quartermaster with no relationship with the Office of the Constructing Quartermaster. The duties and responsibilities of the Constructing Quartermaster stemmed from the Engineering side of the Quartermaster General's Office and not from the side that handled supplies which was to be Major Dill's province at the Field.

Since Major Dill could not report to the Field immediately, it was necessary to have a temporary Quartermaster appointed to arrange for the supplies necessary for the arrival of the first detachments. This temporary appointment was given to Major J. F. Greene who arrived on the Post on the 28th of March to take over those duties during the interval before Major Dill reported.

The last appointment made for Colonel Young's staff was that of Colonel Malcolm C. Grow of the Medical Corps as Post Surgeon. This appointment completed the list of those recommended by General Yount in his February 21st letter to General Arnold. This last appointment was made the third of April 1940, and brought an officer to the Field that had experienced a most remarkable career. Graduating from the Jefferson Medical College in 1909, he had started his military career in 1915, serving in the Russian Army.[13] After the entry of the United States into the War in April of 1917, Colonel Grow transferred to the United States Army, and was commissioned a Captain in the Officers' reserve Corp on the 17th of December, 1917. He was called to active duty on the 15th of April, 1918, thereafter being promoted through the commissioned grades to the rank of Lieutenant Colonel in the Medical Corps of the United States Army, commission that he received on the 3rd of March, 1919. Deciding to remain in the Armed Services, Colonel Grow accepted a commission of Captain in the Medical Corps in the Regular Army granted on the first of March, 1940. Thereafter, he again advanced through the grades of commissioned officers until he was commissioned a Lieutenant Colonel on September 6, 1937, the rank that he held when he was assigned to MacDill Field as the first Base Surgeon. Prior to that time he had specialized in the medical problems peculiar to aviation by taking a course in the Graduate School of Aviation Medicine in 1928, and as a result of flying experience was rated a Flight Surgeon.[14]

Just at the beginning of Colonel Young's regime a change in existing personnel must have caused him some anxiety in view of the fact that it affected the construction program of the field, the most important task confronting the administration of the Field. This personnel change transferred Major Simpson, Constructing Quartermaster for the Field from its inception, to Fort Benning, Georgia on the fifth of March. This was undoubtedly a blow to his brother officers for he, above anyone else, knew and understood the plans for the Field, having sided in preparing the plans undertaken to that date as well as participating in the conferences relating to the Field. As Colonel Lynwood B. Jacobs remarked in the press, "He has worked hard and gotten the job well underway and we would like to have him with us longer."

Fortunately for the Field, Major Simpson had a very capable "understudy" in his offices. This understudy was Captain (soon to be Major) Robert B. Johnston. Captain Johnston had been in the Constructing Quartermaster's Office since the 15th of January when he was transferred from Fort Benning, Georgia.[15] The date of his assignment was early enough so that he was in the Office when the first of the contracts were awarded for the building of the Field. Likewise, he had had time to acquaint himself with the details of the building program that was already in progress. Thus, his appointment would assure a considerable degree of continuity in the important field of construction.

The next problem to occupy Colonel Young's attention after getting his staff together was to prepare to receive the squadrons that were to activate the Field. Of course, it was for this reason that he got the officers together who were necessary to make these arrangements. The plans that had to be developed were: 1.) To arrange the details necessary to enable the units to carry on their function of training combat crews before MacDill Field had either runways or hangars. 2.) To make arrangements to care for the personnel that were to accomplish this function as well as the personnel that were to service the planes and aid in the administration of the Field. 3.) To continue the construction of the Field. The action taken by Colonel Young in the planning and furthering of these aims had to be communicated to Colonel Tinker at Barksdale Field. This was necessary to inform and to receive advice from the Officer who was to be the first permanent commander of the Field.

Next for Colonel Young came the problem of transporting the personnel to and from Tampa. This was essentially a problem for the Officials of the City of Tampa, but it was one that was of great importance to the functioning of the Field. The large number of civilians who were being employed in the construction of the Field had to depend on public transportation. The same was expected to be true of many of the non-commissioned officers who would be permitted to live off the Base. In addition to these dependent on the public transportation, there was to be the usual demands of the enlisted personnel to get back and forth to the City on their free time. So the Base had a very active interest in the establishment of an efficient public transportation system for the convenience of the Base.

The beginning of work on the Base attracted the attention of several companies in the transportation business. Actually, two companies were most aggressive in getting official approval for their respective plans. On the 23rd of December, 1939, the Tamiami Trail Tours announced that they would start service on the MacDill Field Route on Sunday, the 24th of December. They were commencing this operation under a temporary permit granted by the Florida Railroad Commission. That same evening the board of Alderman of the City of Tampa granted temporary authority to Mr. A. B. Grandoff, the Operator of the Tampa Transit Company to operate a similar route. [16]

Obviously political factors were at work as well as business interests. The Tamiami Trail Tours did not commence operations on the 24th of December, as they had announced on the 23rd, but rather on the 4th of January, 1940. These operations by the Tamiami Trail Tours were begun while awaiting the hearing of the Florida Railroad Commission to be held in Tampa on the 11th of January. It developed that the Tamiami Trail Tours was basing its action on the legal ground that the board of Alderman had no jurisdiction over the granting of such a permit as the route was outside the City limits. For that reason the company devoted its attention to the Florida Railroad Commission. [17]

Mr. Grandoff of the Tampa Transit Company took the opposite view, holding that the board of Alderman did have jurisdiction because the Field was in Tampa's Suburban Area. Therefore, Mr. Grandoff made his application to the board of Alderman only. Supporting Mr. Grandoff's opinion of the validity of the Board of Alderman to act in the matter, the streets committee of the board approved Mr. Grandoff's application. This action was taken over the protests of the Tamiami Trail Tours and a company not hitherto mentioned in the proceedings, the Diamond Taxicab Company. [18]

As the hearing of the streets committee of the board of Alderman, the Tamiami Trail Tours again stressed the inadequacy of the board of Alderman to grant a permit running out to the Field, but they also announced that they would file a petition with the board to pick up passengers along the route in Tampa if they received a permit from the railroad commission. The Diamond Taxicab Company, in the person of Mr. Ralph T. Fowery, declared that they had the necessary equipment to care for the additional traffic and had, as well, "full authority to operate in the suburbs." On that basis there was no reason for granting additional permits for the area. With these objectives before it, the committee proceeded to act, but did ask the City Attorney, Mr. McMullen, for a ruling on the right of Tamiami Trail Tours to pick up passengers inside the City under the authority of a railroad commission permit. [19]

While the legal wrangling over jurisdiction continued, the Chamber of Commerce was brought into the picture on the side of Tamiami Trail Tours. The side of this company was presented in an article in the Tampa Tribune, appearing on the 30th of January. This article appealed to public support from Tampa Citizens by pointing out in addition to their superior equipment, they were "rated as a West Coast Organization" with headquarters in Tampa and shops and equipment to service their runs. On the 3rd of January, a committee representing the civic clubs and organizations that was formed to provide housing and recreation facilities for the enlisted men and officers recommended that the Board of Governors of the Chamber of Commerce endorse the service to be provided by Tamiami Trail Tours.[20] This was done by the board of Governors and it further instructed Mr. M. M. Frost to support the petition at the hearing of the State Railroad Commission to be held at Tallahassee on the 11th of January.[21]

Meanwhile, the battle between the two companies for exclusive rights to run a bus line to the Field continued. On the fourth of January the Tamiami Trail Tours formally opened their run[22] and on the ninth of the month the Tampa Transit started its run.[23] On the 10th of January the Board of Alderman granted the Tampa Transit Company the permit that it had been seeking. But this action was taken only after bitter objection had been made by the Tamiami Trail Tours. This protest was accompanied by a petition from the Tamiami Company asking for an exclusive franchise to operate the route inside the city limits and in return give the City of Tampa two and one-half percent of the gross profits. The petition was referred to the streets committee of the board to be considered at a public hearing called for the 15th of January. The protest was based on the contention of Mr. A. Pickens Cole, Attorney for Tamiami Trail Tours, that there was no room in the run to MacDill Field for two bus lines. In other words, the franchise had to be an exclusive one. At the same time, Mr. Cole charged that the Tampa Transit Company was, in reality, owned by the Motor Transit Company of Jacksonville, a company in which the City of Jacksonville owned a minority interest.

Apparently the political problems were thrashed out satisfactorily for the two jurisdictions, the State of Florida and the City of Tampa, for the Board of Alderman accepted the petition of Tamiami Trail Tours and permitted the company to provide bus service inside the City limits. The State Railroad Commission at its hearing in Jacksonville on the 20th of January asserted its right to jurisdiction over the area outside the City limits of Tampa and granted the company a permanent franchise.[24] Tamiami Trail Tours managed to rid itself of competition after it held permits from both authorities by starting injunction proceedings against the Tampa Transit Company. This suit demanded that the rival company should be enjoined from running a bus line to the Field until it had a permit from the State to do so. Since the State Railroad Commission had given Tamiami an exclusive franchise, the result of an injunction would be to rule the Tampa Transit Company from the run entirely.[25] The result of the suit was the granting of the injunction on the 2nd of February. The injunction was granted on the basis that the board of Aldermen did not have the authority to grant a permit for a run outside the city limits of Tampa. Thus, Tamiami Trail Tours became the sole possessors of a franchise to run busses to the field.

There were many advantages in favor of having the bus run in the hands of Tamiami Trail Tours. The fact that the company was affiliated with interstate bus lines guaranteed the listing of MacDill Field as a station of the bus line on the national schedules.[26] Furthermore, the size of the company made it possible to supply equipment and maintenance of the busses that were operated over the route at a time when the conditions of the road made operating expenses particularly high. Yet the service was maintained and made more efficient while carrying passengers from downtown Tampa to the Field for ten cents -- a distance of about nine miles.[27]

Just a week before Colonel Young assumed command of the Field, pending Colonel Tinker's arrival, the first detachment arrived on the field. Their arrival on the 11th of March 1940 aroused Tampa to the realization that an Army Air Corps was actually coming to the field. The Tampa Times ran an eight column headline on page one announcing the arrival of soldiers in the flesh. Actually, only 24 men were in the troop train that pulled into Tampa, the rest coming by automobile, after the custom of troop movements during peace times. Nevertheless, the Tampa papers filled their columns with pictures and news of the men. The troops so feted were brought to Tampa under the command of 1st Lieutenant Robert B. McLelland.[28] The shipment itself coming from Barksdale Field, Shreveport, Louisiana, was to be utilized for clerical working the administrative office, chauffeurs and guards. Upon the arrival of these men, Colonel Jacobs had them settled in the old Quarantine Station at the far end of the peninsula. Here the old quarantine buildings were converted into barracks with a mess hall to provide the living quarters for the men awaiting the completion of the barracks.

The detachment was an advance group of the 27th Air Base Squadron which had been organized on the first of February 1940 at Barksdale Field.[29] This Squadron was organized for the specific purpose of supplying the cadre for the opening of MacDill Field.

With fifty men as earnest of the squadrons and groups to come, the field began to take shape. Although there were no buildings so far completed, work was going along at a sufficiently rapid rate that Colonel Young felt considerable optimism in the ability of the personnel on the base to finish the job in time to take care of the troop shipments still to come. Writing to Colonel Tinker on the 26th of March, he transmitted to him his belief that he would have barracks ready to take care of the men and water and electricity available for use. He had some doubts about the availability of gas and was quite certain that the sewerage system would hardly be ready for the advent of the main body of the 27th Air Base Squadron, due to arrive the middle of April.[30]

The rest of the building program seemed to be getting under way. Captain Johnston announced on the ninth of March that contractors could prepare to submit bids on the base hangar with its shops for general overhaul and repairs, two operating hangars, one Quartermaster warehouse, one Air Corps warehouse, and warming up aprons for the hangars. [31] On the 21st of March it was announced that bids had been asked for construction of a photographic laboratory and a communications building. The communications building was to include a guard house and a fire house. The two buildings were estimated to cost around $100,000. The bids were to be opened on the 18th of April.[32] Then, on the 26th of March, Captain Johnston asked for bids on 4 warehouses that were to cost around $200,000. These warehouses were to include a Quartermaster warehouse, a Quartermaster maintenance warehouse, a Quartermaster warehouse and commissary store building, and a signal and ordnance warehouse. The buildings were scheduled to be 60 feet wide and 140 feet long. The prospective bidders had until two o'clock the afternoon of Wednesday, the 24th of April.

Meantime, the estimates for the hangars had not been announced. Nevertheless, the Office of the Chief of Air Corps was working on the plans. They had held up the submission of the plans and specifications until the funds for its construction would become available on the 30th of June, 1940. Colonel Young was given a preview of these plans from a letter written him by General Arnold. According to General Arnold, the type of building to be used for the hangars was to embody the cyclone proof method of construction of arch roof type. They were to be provided with two story lean-tos, if the concrete structures around the base of the hangars can be called by such an undignified name. The hangars themselves were to include 50,000 square feet of space and were estimated to cost in the neighborhood of $390,000.[33] These were fine plans and when translated into concrete and steel would give MacDill Field some of the finest hangars in the South. But they were to be of little use to opening a field that was to train and maintain combat crews in a few weeks.

As the time for the first unit to arrive to be stationed at MacDill Field was drawing near, Major General H. H. Arnold flew down from Washington for an inspection of the field. This was a short inspection for the purpose of seeing how the work was getting along, for the General arrived at the Peter O'Knight Airport on Friday morning the 12th of April and left for Washington on the morning of the 13th of April. Even in this short time General Arnold had to speak at the annual meeting of the Tampa Chapter of the National Aeronautical Association.[34] There he spoke little of the development of the Field to date, but what he saw was shown to photographers and reporters on a conducted tour of the field.

The newspaper men found themselves at a loss when they were admitted to the field on the 15th of April. It was still too early for the layman to picture the new "Southeastern Air Base". They reported, "The project in too vast". As a result they were forced to quickly abandon their efforts to describe the effect of the building operations and report the progress of the work as told them by the Constructing Quartermaster. They learned that the Government was spending about $5,026,000 on construction with more to come. The temporary barracks were about half finished and that work was under way on the larger permanent structures. Foundations were being dug for warehouses; the non-commissioned officers quarters were rising from the ground and taking shape; ground was being cleared for three hangars; and work was being carried on to remove the muck from the runway area and replace it with sand. [35]

Despite the rawness of the appearance of the Field, both Colonel Young and Captain Johnston were satisfied that they would have plenty of barracks and mess halls to care for the men when they arrived. Their confidence was not misplaced. On Wednesday, the 17th of April, 132 men arrived from Mitchell Field, New York by train. The detachment arrived under the command of Lieutenant Colonel Douglas Johnston. They were immediately set up in the barracks, although gas for the mess halls was not yet available and field kitchens were set up outside the mess halls to cook the food, which was carried inside to the tables. Nor was the sewerage system complete as yet and field sanitary methods had to be used. But the lack of these facilities had been expected for some time and the plans to utilize field methods had been arranged for some time.[36]

On the 24th of April the main body of the 260 men that were assigned to MacDill Field from Barksdale Field arrived in Tampa. The same day, Colonel C. L. Tinker was announced as the new commander of the Field and had arrived in Tampa to check on the progress that had been made. The announcement of the change in command that had been decided upon long before was timed to coincide with the completion of the roster of the 27th Air Base Squadron, which was designed to furnish the personnel for the administration of the base.[37] The number of men on the roster of the 27th Air Base Squadron had now reached 500 men and the Field could be said to be activated. In keeping with this step, it was fitting that the man who had been put in charge of making the arrangements for the squadron and had been acting as its commanding officer before its arrival, and was going to continue as such until Colonel Tinker assumed command, should be promoted. On the 19th day of April Lieutenant Colonel Young was informed that he had been promoted to the rank of full Colonel.[38]

Now that the 27th Air Base Squadron was housed and at work, it was necessary to get things ready for the tactical squadrons to be brought to the Field to carry out the mission of the Field. These squadrons were to make up the 29th Bombardment Group (Heavy) that was to be assigned to the field when it was ready for them, and it was expected that they would be brought to the Field in May.

Obviously the condition of the field would not permit it to be in shape to care for the planes that would arrive with the 29th Group. Some other arrangements had to be made and plans had been underway for some time to do just that. But even so, the long range importance of those plans probably did not occur to the planners.

This temporary plan that was arranged to care for the flying requirements of the 29th Group was to utilize the almost abandoned municipal airport known as Drew Field. This field had been set up as the Airport for the City of Tampa, but the completion of the Peter O'Knight Airport on Davis Island, which brought the Airport facilities closer to the center of the city, brought an end to its usefulness. From that time on, the city had maintained the field as an auxiliary landing field.[39] Despite the fact that the field had practically been abandoned, the turf covering provided a sufficiently solid foundation to permit ships as large as the four engine B-17s to land and takeoff. Therefore, the Army Air Force decided to lease it from the City on a short term basis.

This plan was evolved and presented to the City as far back as the 28th of March and, indeed, the first plane assigned to MacDill Field landed at Drew Field on that date. Not much work was expanded on the field for the reason of the short period that it was expected to be used at the time. However, the electric wires that had skirted the north side of the field were removed by the Tampa Electric Company.[40] It should be noted that the line was removed by the company according to Colonel Young "without hesitation, without delay, and at their own expense."[41]

The lease itself was signed on the 22nd of April and forwarded to Washington. After the lease was signed, the plans called for tents to be erected for 200 men.[42] The men who were to be stationed at Drew Field were there on detached service for a period of two weeks. Then they were to be brought back to MacDill Field and another group was to be sent in its place. The men, while on duty at Drew Field, were to be the ground force maintaining the planes.

Meanwhile, the headquarters were moved out to the Base from the City Hall in Tampa. On the 26th of March, Colonel Young wrote Colonel Tinker of his plans to move the headquarters to the Field as soon as the 27th Air Base Squadron arrived. To do this Colonel Young took over the north row of barracks for his headquarters, with Signal Ordinance, Quartermaster, and other service offices in the barracks to the east of the Base Headquarters and the 29th Bomb Group Headquarters in the barracks to the west of the Base Headquarters.[43] This plan was inaugurated by Colonel Young's office, moving from the City Hall on the 16th of April. Captain Robert B. Johnston soon followed suit by moving the Construction Quartermaster's offices to the field. This building that was destined to become the resident Engineers Office near the Bayshore Gate was the one to which these latter offices were moved.[44]

After the establishment of the Base Headquarters on the Field, Colonel Young found two big problems that had to be settled. One of these was the procurement of additional officers for staffing the Base Administration Offices. Colonel Young requested Colonel Tinker to get in touch with the Personnel Division while he was in Washington to decide upon officers that could take over duties connected with the offices to be filled. These offices were: Finance Agent, Adjutant, Operations, Post Exchange and Transportation. He suggested the three officers who came with the 27th Air Base Squadron from Barksdale Field might be utilized to fill some of these vacancies. But even if these could be assigned to fill some of the duties mentioned, it would be necessary to have officers who could take care of the squadrons.[45]

The second problem that Colonel Young had to face was the change in the hospital plans. When General Arnold had made his inspection trip to the field on the 12th of April[46], he had directed that the hospital be transferred from the Old Quarantine Station to a location several hundred yards north of the present location of the Officer's Club. This would have placed it on the water front somewhere near the present location of the docks.[47] This location would have brought the hospital much closer to the barracks area than the Quarantine Station that had originally been decided upon as the site of the hospital. However, certain practical difficulties presented themselves. The area that General Arnold suggested as the site for the hospital was swampy and would require a great deal of fill to make it usable. Then too, the proximity of the barracks area on the one side and the flying field on the other would make the location far more noisy than the Quarantine Station site.

TAMPA
(099-777I-21R)(11-28-40-10:00A)(12·500) BOMB GROUP CAMP, DREW FIELD, TAMPA, FLA.

(0127-777I-21R)(1-28-41-3:00P)(12-600) CONSTRUCTION, DREW FIELD, FLA.

(0126-777I-21R)(1-28-41-3:15P)(12-600) CONSTRUCTION, DRE

(08·792J·21R)(2·19·41·10:28A)(12·200) HOSPITAL, AIR CORPS BASE, ORLANDO, FLA.

To these objections Colonel Young added two very solid criticisms of the proposed move. The work required to erect a hospital at the proposed site would take a great deal of time to accomplish. Meanwhile, the hospital facilities maintained at the Quarantine Station would have to be kept to a minimum due to the temporary character of the establishment there. This would retard the establishment of a complete hospital for the Base. Furthermore, the cost of transferring the site of the hospital would entail the spending of approximately a half million dollars. If this expenditure could be converted into a saving which in turn could be expended for equipment, it would mean a much finer installation for the Base. Consequently, Colonel Young and Colonel Grow were emphatically in favor of leaving the site of the hospital in its original location.[48]

Despite the objections raised, plans were made in accordance with General Arnold's suggestion and the only thing possible to prevent the completion of these plans was to get the matter reconsidered. For this reason Colonel Young wrote to Colonel Tinker, who was in Washington at the Office of the Chief of the Air Corps, holding conferences on the development and future of MacDill Field prior to his assuming active command.[49] This was very fortunate for progress of the Field, as Colonel Tinker could personally talk the matter over with General Arnold and others of his staff. This avenue for the presentation of the ideas of those on the ground at MacDill Field proved effective and the site of the hospital remained as originally planned.

Colonel Young was now approaching the end of his first administration of the MacDill Field. He was destined to guide the destinies of the Field at various periods in its later history, but this first administration probably called for more originality on his part than any of the others. It had been his duty to make the arrangements for the reception of the first squadron to be housed on the Field; he had to break the way for the establishment of relationships with the civil authorities in Tampa; he had been charged with the task of acquainting the skeleton staff that was assigned to the Field with the work to be done; he had to make the arrangements for the use of Drew Field as a flying field for the tactical squadrons. All this had to be done in such a way that the permanent Commanding Officer, Colonel Tinker, could assume control smoothly and efficiently. The gauge of his success as the temporary Commanding Officer of the Field was the ease with which Colonel Tinker took over the command and continued the activities of the Field.

REFERENCES

1. SO #47, WD Washington, 26 February 1940.
2. Ibid, Tampa Tribune, 28 February 1940.
3. Tampa Tribune, 2 March 1940.
4. Army Register, 1943.
5. Tampa Tribune, 2 March 1940.
6. Interview with Colonel Young, 4 February 1944.
7. See Chapter II, page 2.
8. Letter from Brigadier General Barton K. Yount to Major General H. H. Arnold, 21 February 1940, Paragraph 10.
9. Letter from Colonel H. H. Young to Major John P. Sparks, Office of Military Attaché, The American Embassy, London, 25 August 1941 -- copy in 201 File H. H. Young.
10. SO #2, AB Headquarters, MacDill Field, 21 March 1940.
11. Tampa Tribune, 21 March 1940.
12. The Army Register, 1943, page 236.
13. Tampa Tribune, 25 May 1940.
14. Officers Army Register, 1943.
15. Tampa Tribune, 5 March 1940.
16. Tampa Tribune, 23 December 1939.
17. Tampa Tribune, 26 January 1940.
18. Tampa Tribune, 5 January 1940.
19. Tampa Tribune, 5 January 1940.
20. Tampa Tribune, 3 January 1940.
21. Tampa Tribune, 5 January 1940.
22. Tampa Tribune, 5 January 1940.
23. Tampa Tribune, 10 January 1940.
24. Tampa Tribune, 21 January 1940.
25. Tampa Tribune, 26 January 1940.
26. Tampa Tribune, 21 January 1940.
27. Historical data supplied by Colonel Young.
28. Tampa Times, 11 March 1940 and Tampa Tribune, 12 March 1940.
29. GO #1, AB Headquarters, Barksdale Field, 18 January 1940.
30. Letter Colonel Young to Colonel Tinker, Barksdale Field, 26 March 1940, 201 File H. H. Young.
31. Tampa Tribune, 9 March 1940.
32. Tampa Tribune, 21 March 1940.

33. Letter to Colonel H. H. Young, MacDill Field Headquarters, from Major General H. H. Arnold, Office of the Chief of Air Corps, 23 April 1940.
34. Tampa Tribune, 13 April 1940.
35. Tampa Tribune, 16 April 1940.
36. 201 File, Young, H. H., Letter from Colonel H. H. Young to Colonel Tinker, 26 March 1940.
37. Tampa Tribune, 24 April 1940.
38. SO #93, AAF Headquarters, Washington, D. C., 19 April 1940.
39. Tampa Tribune, 27 April 1940.
40. See A. R. Hathaway's answer to General Arnold's request for removal made during his speech to the National Aeronautic Association. Tampa Tribune, 17 April 1940.
41. Historical Data provided by Colonel H. H. Young.
42. Tampa Tribune, 2 May 1940.
43. 201 File, Young, H. H., Letter from Colonel Young to Colonel C. L. Tinker, 26 March 1940.
44. Tampa Tribune, 4 May 1940.
45. 201 File, Young, H. H. Letter, Colonel Young to Colonel Tinker, Washington, D. C., 20 April 1940.
46. Tampa Tribune, 13 April 1940.
47. 201 File, Young, H. H., Letter Colonel C.L. Tinker, Office of the Chief of Air Corps, Washington, D. C., dated 20 April 1940.
48. 201 File Young, H. H., Letter from Colonel Young to Colonel C. L. Tinker, Office of the Chief of Air Corps, Washington, D. C., dated 20 April 1940.
49. Ibid.

Colonel Clarence L. Tinker
Assumes command of MacDill Field
17 May 1940

CHAPTER V

COLONEL TINKER'S ADMINISTRATION (1ST PHASE)

The week beginning Wednesday the 16th of May, 1940 represents the opening date of MacDill Field as an operational training field. On Wednesday the planes arrived that were assigned to the 29th Bombardment Group (H). On Thursday Colonel Tinker arrived to take command of the Field. During the rest of the week enlisted personnel making up the 29th Group arrived on the Field, with the majority coming in on Tuesday, the 22nd of the month. These events pointed up the fact that the Field, even though it was far from completion, had advanced to the point in its construction program where it was ready to be launched on the career for which it was designed.

The arrival of Colonel Tinker brought to the Field the first commanding officer that was to be in charge of and directly responsible for the policies that were to govern the activities of the Base. Prior to his arrival the two men who had been referred to as the commanding officers had held that title with the understanding that it was only a temporary arrangement pending the permanent appointment. Their work had largely consisted of supervising the construction work in its early stages, carrying that work along to the point where the Field was ready to receive the organizations that were to put it on an operational basis. Even before Colonel Young was sent to the Field in March it was known that Colonel Tinker would eventually take command of the Field as soon as the transfer of his duties at Barksdale Field, where he was Group Commander, could be completed.[1] This situation meant that decisions made on the Field had to be in accordance with Colonel Tinker's own plans for its future development. This, of course, necessitated trips to the Field[2] as well as correspondence communicating the decisions that had been made and the requirements needed for the Field.[3] Now that the permanent commander was in residence on the Field decisions affecting it could be taken immediately.

The new Commanding Officer was a man with broad experience in the Army. Born in Indian Territory in Oklahoma in 1888, Colonel Tinker started his military career when he was enrolled in the Wentworth Military Academy. Upon his graduation from the Academy in 1908 he received a commission as a Third Lieutenant in the Philippine Constabulary. In 1912 he was commissioned a second Lieutenant in the Infantry of the United States Army. With the coming of the war, Colonel Tinker's rise in the ranks of commissioned officer in the infantry was rapid, being a Major when the war ended. Retaining his commission as Major in the Regular Army after the war in 1920, he was stationed at Polytechnic College, Riverside, California as Professor of Military Science and Tactics. He transferred to the Air Service in 1921 after taking his flying training at Fort Sill, Oklahoma. In 1926 Colonel Tinker graduated from the Command and General Staff School in Fort Leavenworth, and in the preceding year he completed the course given in the Air Service Tactical School. Other courses involving aeronautics taken by Colonel Tinker included that given by the Air Service Observation School, where he graduated in 1921 and the Air service Tactical School which he completed in 1925.

In addition to an intensive schooling for his profession, Colonel Tinker had had wide experience ranging from Commander of the Air Service Troops at Fort Riley, Kansas, a member of the Staff of the Chief of the Air Corps, Commander of Hamilton Field, California, and Assistant Military Attaché in the United States Embassy in London. It was while he was Assistant Attaché in London that Colonel Tinker was awarded the Soldier's Medal. A plane crashed that Colonel Tinker (then Major) was piloting. In spite of the fact that he himself was injured, Colonel Tinker affected the rescue of the passengers of the plane, which had burst into flames, disregarding his own injuries and personal safety. Furthermore, Colonel Tinker had commanded a flight of bombers from Hamilton Field, California, to Washington, D.C., in 1935. The time of 14 1/2 hours that it took for the flight was a record for formation flying at that time. Thus the new commander of the newest operational base was a man with great experience in flying, administration and leading men.

The Staff that was to aid Colonel Tinker in the administration of the new field was, to a large extent, already in operation when he arrived with the troops on the 17th of May 1940. Colonel Young was retained as his Executive Officer and S-2 Officer.[4] Major Barnett was transferred from Air Corps Supply to the Office of Adjutant and S-1. Major Skow, who had been transferred from Langley Field, Virginia, on the 14th of May 1940, was put in charge of S-3. The first Commanding Officer of the Field, Colonel Lynwood B. Jacobs, was made the first S-4 of the Field to add to his rather imposing list of firsts that he gathered at MacDill Field. Some of the Service Officers were also on the field prior to Colonel Tinker's advent as the Commanding Officer. Colonel Malcolm C. Grow the Base Surgeon, and Major Louis Canaler, the Signal Officer of the Base since January, 1940. Major J. F. Greene was still awaiting the arrival of Major Lois C. Dill to relieve him of his temporary assignment as Base Quartermaster. With these officers, all of them men with broad and varied experience in their respective assignments, Colonel Tinker had a group well suited to aid him in the development of the new Air Base even if they represented only a skeleton staff.

The first task that Colonel Tinker and his staff had to handle was the reception of the 29th Bombardment Group (H), led by Lieutenant Colonel Vincent J. Meloy, Commanding Officer. The arrival of this group from Langley Field brought Tampa a realization of the meaning of being an "army town". The arrival of the troop train bringing 350 officers and enlisted men gave Tampans their first view of the Army in the mass. Crowds of excited citizens came down to see the boys come in. Some of them probably had nostalgic twinges of trains that carried troops in other wars. At any rate, the soldiers and the girls were much the same as they had always been, even if it were times of peace, and the calls that followed the girls seemed to indicate that it was only a matter of getting some free time before the boys would be in Tampa trying to find them.

The authorization of the transfer of the 29th Bombardment Group was sent to the Commanding General of the General Headquarters Air Force at Langley Field, Virginia on the 8th of May. The authorization stipulated the equipment that the organization was to carry with it at that time. This equipment is of interest because it testifies to the newness of the MacDill field and the consequent lack of supplies. This list included such articles as beds, mattresses, pillows and sheets. It also included post camp and station equipment that might be "surplus to the needs of Langley Field and required for initial operations at MacDill field". Such equipment, usually furnished by the Field that was to receive the organization, simply wasn't on hand at MacDill Field.[5]

Plans were made to conform with these orders and on the 10th of May Lieutenant Colonel Vincent Meloy wrote to his friend, Lieutenant Colonel Harry H. Young, giving him the outline of the preparations that had been made. According to this plan, and it was substantially followed, the air echelon was to arrive at Drew Field on the morning of the 15th, bringing 53 enlisted men to MacDill Field. The officers concerned in this flight were to return to Langley Field. At the same time the air echelon was to bring three B-17s and two A-17s that were to be left at Drew Field for the use of the Group. The next group to leave Langley Field was the motor convoy.

It was planned that the convoy should leave for MacDill on the 15th under the command of Lieutenant Bond and it was scheduled to arrive at the Field on the 18th. A detail was to be dispatched to Henderson, North Carolina to pick up the tractors and tank trailers necessary for the operation of Drew Field and leave Henderson for MacDill field on the 16th.The date of arrival was not specified. The troop train, carrying the balance of the men who were not authorized to use private transportation, were scheduled to leave Langley Field at 1447 hours on the 20th and arrive at Port Tampa about 1530 hours on the 21st. Colonel Meloy was going to make the trip on the troop train, taking command of that phase of the movement of the 29th Group. Accompanying him was to be Major Asp, Major Old and Captain Gould.[6] Captain Gould was a medical officer stationed at Langley Field and was accompanying the movement as the Train Surgeon and was to return to his station on the completion of the trip.[7] This plan was confirmed by telegram from Colonel West, the commanding officer of the Air Base Headquarters at Langley Field, on the 10th of May. The only change in time being that the troop train was supposed to arrive in Tampa at 1320, the 21st May.

According to plan, the orders were cut to permit the motor convoy to leave on the 15th of May.[8] At the same time, the detail that was to go to Henderson, North Carolina was ordered to leave on the 15th of May as well.[9] This order was amended that next day to delay the start of this detail until the 16th.[10] It was expected that the trip for this detail would take about ten days in reaching MacDill.[11] The same Special Orders ordered the enlisted men of the 29th Bombardment Group to be shipped by train or private conveyance on the 15th or "as soon thereafter as is practicable". Actually the shipment left Langley Field on the 21st of May, arriving in Tampa the evening of the 22nd of May.

Originally the routing of the trip had planned to make use of the direct route between Hampton, Virginia and Tampa. By this route it was hoped to arrive in Tampa by 1:30 on the 22nd of May. Instead the Quartermaster General approved a route through Danville, Virginia which took them off the fast passenger route and landed them in Tampa about 7 o'clock in the evening. This necessitated the addition of an extra baggage car to carry the field ranges that had to be set up to feed the men. The route also made the trip slow. In addition to this, the lack of air conditioning and the hot weather made it necessary for the windows to be opened, and the men arrived in a condition that one described as making him look as if he had "fired the boilers on the way down." Faulty loadings also added to the difficulties of the trip because the loads in two of the three baggage cars shifted and set the emergency brakes. Finally, the Quartermaster had not purchased enough upper birth tickets to make it possible to keep the organizations intact and reorganization of cars had to take place while the trip was in progress. When all was bedded down for the evening, enlisted men were bunked in with officers so as to give them a bed to sleep in the war years when troops were moved, possibly because all officers involved in a troop movement are not apprised of the conditions surrounding the particular movement. At any rate, the 29th Bomb Group arrived in Tampa hot, tired and dirty, quite pleased to get off the train and make camp where best they could.

The 29th Bomb Group had been formed at Langley Field on the first of February for the express purpose of carrying on the operations at MacDill Field. The Group was composed of three squadrons that were formed on that date for the purpose of carrying out the mission of the group. These squadrons were the 82nd, the 6th and the 42rd. The enlisted personnel that made up these squadrons were transferred to it for the most part from the 49th Squadron of the Second Bombardment Group (H) that was stationed at Langley Field.[12] The rest of the men came from Pope Field to complete the roster. The men that made up the personnel of these organizations were the gunners and radio operators of the combat crews and the technicians that assigned to the ground crews caring for the maintenance of the planes. The rest of the men came from Pope Field to complete the roster. The men that made up the personnel of these organizations were the gunners and radio operators of the combat crews and the technicians that were assigned to the ground crews caring for the maintenance of the planes.

The Commander of the 29th Group, Lieutenant Colonel Vincent J. Meloy, was an example of the broad experience and fine training that had been given the officers entrusted with the initial work on MacDill Field. Colonel Meloy had entered the service as a private in the 1st Aero Squadron of the New York National Guard on the first of September 1916. He took his flying training in the Aviation Section of the Signal Corps and received his pilot's wings in December 1917. He was made a First Lieutenant in the Aviation Section of the Signal Corps, Officers Reserve Corps on the 31st of December, 1917 and called to active duty on the 2nd of January, 1918. In 1920 he was made a Second Lieutenant and First Lieutenant on the First of July, 1920 in the Air Services. Just prior to his assignment as Group Commander of the 29th, Colonel Meloy had been advanced to the temporary rank of Lieutenant Colonel. The education of Colonel Meloy, who was born in Brooklyn, New York, included attendance at Vanderbilt University in Kentucky and The Massachusetts Institute of Technology in Boston. In 1934 he graduated from the Command and General Staff School at Fort Leavenworth Kansas. Upon his graduation from the Command and General Staff School he was assigned to Langley Field as Commander of the20th Bomb Group. In 1938 Colonel Meloy received nation-wide attention when he commanded the good will flight of the Air Corps to South America when three B-17s flew to Bogotá, Columbia and Buenos Aires,

Argentina.[13] The staff assembled to direct the activities of the 29th Bomb Group consisted of men with wide experience in the field of aviation.

His executive officer, Major Melvin B. Asp, now Colonel Asp, had entered the Army through the Infantry of the National Guard as a Sergeant in Company I, 1st Infantry of Minnesota. On the 8th of December, 1917 he transferred to the Aviation Section of the Signal Corps, going back to a Private First Class in order to make the transfer. He took his flying training at that time and was accepted as a Second Lieutenant in May 1918 and was called to duty at the same time. He was granted a regular Second Lieutenant's Commission at the conclusion of the War on the 20th of July 1920. He graduated from the Air Corps Tactical School in 1939, and was assigned to Langley Field, Virginia, from which he was transferred to MacDill Field. This last appointment was a very happy one for Major Asp for his parents were making their home in Sarasota, and he himself had attended the Tampa public schools.[14]

In addition to Major Asp, Colonel Meloy had Major Cornelius E. O'Connor, a graduate of West Point in the 1917 class as his material officer. Captain Edwin L. Tucker, a graduate from the Flight Training School at Kelly Field in 1929 was brought from Langley Field, Virginia, as operations officer.

First Lieutenant Harry B. Melton, Colonel Meloy's adjutant, was a graduate of West Point in the Class of 1932. Entering active service in the Cavalry, he transferred to the Air Corps in January 1938 and was promoted to the rank of First Lieutenant in June, 1939. Major (temporary) Walter G. Bryte had just been advanced from Captain in March before he came to MacDill Field to take over his duties as the Commanding Officer of the Headquarters and Headquarters Squadron under Colonel Meloy. Major Bryte was another graduate of West Point, graduating in the Class of 1921. He had gone directly into the Air Service and had attended the various flying schools that trained him as a specialist in aviation. His flying experience had been such that he was rated as a Command Pilot, a Command Observer and an Air Observer. Prior to coming to MacDill Field he had been president of the Third Corps Area Flying Cadet Procurement Board. Thus Colonel Meloy had an experienced group of officers to fill the staff positions of his command and were to prove their competency in operational training in the coming months.[15] The commanding officers of the Squadrons were likewise experienced Army men. Major Hugo P. Rush, who had graduated from West Point in June of 1918, and had received his temporary majority in July 1939, was selected as commanding officer of the 6th Squadron. Major William D. Old was selected as the commanding officer of the 29th Squadron. He was an officer that had entered the Army as a Second Lieutenant after his graduation from Texas College of Agricultural and Mechanical Arts in 1924 with the degree of Bachelor of Science in Electrical Engineering. He had entered the Army in the Air Service and had received his flight training in the Air Service Schools, receiving his pilot's rating in 1925. He also graduated from the General Staff and Command School in Fort Leavenworth in 1931 and the Air Corps Tactical School in 1936. His flying experience after receiving his pilot's rating had brought him the ratings of Command Pilot, Command Observer, and Air Observer. He had advanced through the ranks of commissioned officers to the commission of Major (temporary) which he had received just before coming to MacDill Field in March 1940.[16] The 52nd Squadron was commanded by Captain Frank H. Robinson. This officer had entered the Army as a Flying Cadet in 1926. After completing his flying training he continued in the Army, graduating from Advanced Flying School and Observation Course in 1927. Captain Robinson's flying experience had brought him the coveted ratings of Senior Pilot, Command Observer and Air Observer. He received his commission as Captain in June 1937.

REFERENCES

1. Letter from Brigadier General B. K. Yount to Major General H. H. Arnold, dated 21 February 1940.
2. i.e., Inspection trip, Tampa Tribune, 25 April 1940 and visit of 1 May 1940, Young, H. H. 201 File, Telegram 29 April 1940.
3. Letters of Colonel Young to Colonel Tinker, H. H. Yong, 26 March 1940 and 20 April 1940.
4. Tampa Tribune, 25 April 1940.
5. AG 370.5 (4-24-1940) AGO May 8, 1940. Subject: Movement of 29th Bombardment Group to MacDill Field. To: The Commanding General, GHQ AF, Langley Field, Virginia.
6. (370.5) Letter headquarters 29th Bombardment Group (H), Langley Field, May 10, 1940. To: Lieutenant Colonel Harry H. Young, MacDill Field, Florida.
7. SO #114, AB Headquarters Langley Field, Virginia, May 14, 1940, Paragraph 4.
8. SO #49, Headquarters, 29th Bombardment Group (H) GHQ AF, Langley Field, Virginia, Paragraph 2, May 14, 1940.
9. Ibid, Paragraph 2.
10. SO #50, Headquarters 29th Bombardment Group (H) GHQ AF, Langley Field, May 15, 1940, Paragraph 1.
11. SO #49, Headquarters 29th bombardment Group (H) GHQ AF, Langley Field, May 14, 1940, Paragraph 2.
12. Interview with CWO Richard C. Keller.
13. Tampa Tribune, 24 February, 12 and 22 May 1940, Tampa Times, 1 July 1940 and Army Register, 1943.
14. Tampa Tribune, 12 May 1940, Army Register, 1943, and Asp, Melvin B., 201 File.
15. Tampa Tribune, 24 February and 12 May 1940.
16. Tampa Tribune, 24 February 1940.

CHAPTER VI

SERVICE UNITS AT MACDILL IN 1940

The establishment of an Air Corps base such as MacDill field required the services of more units than an Air Base Squadron and a tactical group. These other units, known as service units, had been dispatched in some cases before the arrival of the 29th bomb Group because their services were so vitally necessary to the proper functioning of the Base. One of the first of these units was the Medical Department Detachment. Colonel Tinker had requested that five Medical Corps enlisted men be included in the detachment of the 27th Air Base Squadron that arrived the 11th of March.[1] Possibly because orders had to issue from a source other than the Air Base Headquarters at Barksdale Field, the medical detachment did not arrive with the first group under 1st Lieutenant McClellan, but came on the 15th of March, four days later.[2] This first group consisted of a sergeant and three privates. In order to care for the medical needs of the whole 27th Air Base Squadron, 16 men were dispatched from Langley Field on the 1st of April, arriving on the field the 2nd of April.[3] This group included a Technical Sergeant, a sergeant and a corporal.[4] The first medical officer to arrive on the field came with the Base Headquarters and the 27th Air Base Squadron on the 24th of April. This officer, 1st Lieutenant Sidney J. Nethery, Jr., Medical Resident, was later appointed the first War Officer for the Station Hospital by Lieutenant Colonel Malcolm C. Grow, who had only arrived on the Field himself on the 4th of April[5]. To this complement, was added the entire Medical Department Detachment that had been set up at Barksdale Field for the Southeastern Air Base. This group consisted of 28 privates, but with them were transferred the allotment of grades and ratings to MacDill Field that had been assigned the detachment when it was set up.[6]

The work assigned to the Medical Detachment before the arrival of the medical staff was to prepare the buildings and receive the equipment for the hospital that was planned for the base. This work was so important that the Headquarters for the General Headquarters Air Force felt that the hospital facilities should be provided before the 29th Bombardment Group could be moved to the Field.[7]

Prior to the hospital installation, the medical service that was rendered on the Field had to be confined to dispensary service. At first this was done in a room set aside for the purpose in the Quarantine Station. Then on the 15th of May a Base infirmary was established in the Barracks Area where it was more convenient for the men.[8] Serious cases requiring hospitalization were to be sent to the Veterans Hospital according to the first arrangements.[9] But apparently arrangements were made with the Tampa Municipal Hospital to care for some of the cases at least, for that hospital did receive some cases from the Field as late as May 27, 1940.[10] However that might have been, the Hospital continued to develop all during the summer so that by the end of August the authorities were able to report that they were able to offer all of the services necessary for a well established hospital.

The Signal Corps units so necessary to the proper functioning of the Air Corps, have a somewhat hazy beginning on MacDill Field due to the lack of certain records. A detachment of the 5th Signal Service Company is reported to have been on the field as early as the 30th of March[11], but newspaper accounts at the time report Major Louis Cansler, the first Signal Officer on the Field, as expecting the arrival of five men. Possibly Major Cansler was expecting reinforcements for the men that had already been sent. The first report of a Signal Corps Detachment that has been found is carried in the Venereal Report for the period ending April 26, 1940. [12] The first official notice of Signal Corps activity at MacDill Field that has been found is contained in a letter from the Adjutant General's Office, dated May 16, 1940. According to this letter the Commanding General of the Fourth Corps Area was authorized to enlist 22 men for the Ninth Signal Platoon to ship them to MacDill Field. The letter urged that the recruiting be pushed as rapidly as possible and to complete the quota by the 1st of July, if not completed by that date, the quota was to be carried over to subsequent requisitions.[13] Recruits for this organization began appearing on the Field on the 27th of May, and were attached to the Detachment 5th Signal Service Company.[14] This method of attaching recruits to the 5th Signal Detachment continued until the 12th of June when the men were relieved from attachment to that organization [15] and were ordered to report to their commanding officer, Major Louis Cansler who had just received the command of that organization in addition to his other duties.[16] The date of the activation of the 9th Signal Platoon was made effective as of the 1st June 1940.[17] At this time the Platoon consisted of one Sergeant, one Corporal and 22 Privates. This organization was not destined to a long career for on the 19th of September its personnel and equipment were transferred, together with cadres that had been attached to the 304th Signal Aviation Company, to the 312th and 317th Signal Aviation Companies which were activated at MacDill Field the 19th of September.[18] These two organizations took the place of the 9th Signal Platoon that was accordingly disbanded. The 317th Signal Aviation Company was activated to form the company that was to go to Morrison Field, West Palm Beach. The 312th Signal Aviation Company, with a strength of 71 men was to stay at MacDill Field.[19]

The Detachment Quartermaster Corps, like the Signal Corps Detachment, is an early organization whose records are not now available. The records show that this Detachment had an actual strength of three men on the 26th of April 1940.[20] Aside from this report there are no records that give any indication concerning their arrival at MacDill Field. The first group of men to man the Quartermaster Offices on the Base for which there is a record, were sent as a result of a letter from the Headquarters of the Fourth Corps Area to the Commanding Officer of the Air Base Headquarters of Barksdale field on the 23rd of April. This letter instructed that officer to issue orders to send twenty-eight privates that had been attached to the Detachment Quartermaster Corps at Barksdale Field to MacDill Field. These orders were issued the 27th of April and ordered the men to leave Barksdale on or about May 2nd.[21] Additional men for the Detachment were sent to MacDill Field from Langley Field, leaving there the 16th of May, 1940. This latter shipment included two sergeants and one corporal in addition to one specialist second class and one specialist fifth class. The arrival of non-commissioned officers was probably received with great appreciation at the Field, for they were so short of experienced men that the Fourth Corps Area put out a special letter advertising a list of vacancies in the Quartermaster personnel for the Field. According to this letter, dated the 29th of April, there was need for four sergeants, one corporal and eleven privates first class. The letter ordered the Commanding Officers of posts in the Area to give their personnel with the appropriate rank an opportunity to transfer to MacDill. Furthermore enlisted men of lower grade were permitted to make application to be considered for the vacancies.[22]

The first regularly organized Quartermaster Units to be established on the Field were activated the 11th of June, 1940. These units were the Quartermaster Company 238 (Sep), Company "F", 30th Quartermaster Regiment (Truck) and a detachment of Company "B", 89th Quartermaster Battalion (Light Maintenance).[23] These units superseded the Base Quartermaster Detachment and absorbed the personnel of the former unit in accordance with their duties. The duties that each of these new units performed and which dictated the disposal of the older unit's personnel were as follows: The Quartermaster Company 238 (Sep) took charge of commissary and supply; company F, 30th Quartermaster Regiment (Truck) took charge of Quartermaster transportation; and Company "B", 89th Quartermaster Battalion took charge of truck maintenance and repair.

These units remained on the Field for some time, although Company B sent a detachment of 18 men to Orlando on the activation of the Air Base there. (SO #163, MacDill Field 12 November 1940, Paragraph 15.) In August another reorganization took place and two more Quartermaster Units were added to the unit roster of the Field. These two units were the 244th Separate Quartermaster Company (Air Base) and the 245th Separate Quartermaster Company (Air Base).[24] Each of these units were to become effective as of midnight the 16th of August, 1940, with 100 men each. The two units, as their name indicates, were organized as Air Base Units. For that reason then, the 245th was assigned to serve MacDill Field, while the 244th was transferred to the newly activated Orlando Air Base late in September, 1940.[25]

The Quartermaster Corps sent the first colored troops to MacDill field. These men made up the personnel of Company "G" of the 31st Quartermaster Regiment (Trk). A Cadre for this organization was sent from Company "L" of the 48th Quartermaster Regiment, stationed at Fort Benning Georgia, arriving at MacDill field at 10:30 AM on the 25th of August, 1940.[26]

The other companies of the 31st Quartermaster Regiment (Truck), Company "F" and Company "G" are officially recorded as being on the Field during September, October and November.[27] Company "B" of the 88th Quartermaster Battalion is also recorded for the same three months.[28] In all three of these cases no records are available that would indicate when these organizations were activated or received on the Field.

The work to be done by the 29th Bombardment Group also required certain services of a technical nature that required special organizations to care for them and which began to move to the Field when the Group was domiciled there. One of the first of these specialized units that were needed when the tactical organizations came to the Field, was an Ordnance Company. This organization was the 336th Ordnance Company of the 52nd Ordnance Battalion. Originally the unit had been stationed at Langley Field and activated as the 10th Ordnance Company and redesignated the 51st Battalion was to be broken up into three companies and sent to permanent stations at MacDill Field, McChord Field, Washington, and Moffett Field, California. According to this letter of instruction, the 336th Company that was to be sent to MacDill Field was to consist of 23 enlisted men. Of these nine were to be sent to Barksdale Field to accompany the 29th Bomb Group when it moved to MacDill Field, the others to be sent later. Amendments to the letter of instruction provided that 24 men were to be sent with the Group and these were ordered to leave Langley Field on the 20th of May, 1940.[30] These men arrived at Barksdale Field too late to accompany the movement of the 29th Bomb Group as they didn't get there until the 23rd of May. Additional orders at Barksdale were issued that started these men to MacDill Field driving trucks to be used by the Ordnance Company. The convoy set out on the 3rd of June and their routing plans called for them to arrive in Tampa on the 6th of that month.[31] In September of 1940 this organization was augmented by the addition of 66 enlisted men from the Ordnance Department assigned to the Air Base at Langley Field.[32] This transfer was made effective the 1st of October, 1940, there being five sergeants, 16 corporals, 28 privates first class and 17 privates involved in the transfer.

The Weather Detachment was started at MacDill field when men from the 2nd and 3rd Weather Squadrons were sent in to set up the weather station at Drew Field. The first man to arrive for this duty was Staff Sergeant Ben Greenberg, 6710629, of the 2nd Weather Squadron, Lawson Field, Fort Benning, Georgia, who reported on the 24th of May 1940.[33] The majority of the men for this unit were sent in by the Third Weather Squadron to carry on the work for the operations of the 29th Group from Drew Field,[34] and were subsequently given permanent assignments to the Field and attached for messing and administration and quarters to the Base Headquarters and 27th Air Base Squadron(S). With the reorganization of the 27th Air Base Squadron as the 27th Air Base Group, the enlisted personnel were attached to the Detachment 3rd Weather Squadron, Air Corps, effective September 1, 1940. Since there were only eight men in the detachment, it was found impossible to carry on the duties of an individual unit, and Detachment Commander, 1st Lieutenant R. E. Beebe requested that they be reattached to Base headquarters Squadron in order to take care of the administration work that was involved for a separate orgnization.[35] Since the duties of this unit were to provide weather information for the flights of the 29th Group, and since flying operations during 1940 were carried on exclusively at Drew Field, the men were permanently stationed there, not taking residence at MacDill Field proper until the Field was ready to carry on flight operations from its own airdrome.

One of the innovations launched by the Air Corps in 1940 was to provide itself with Engineering Units to take charge of the construction of flying fields and other construction activity necessary to the Air Corps. One of the first Air Bases to receive these units was MacDill Field. A letter of instruction from the Adjutant General's Office, dated the 25th of may, 1940, made June 1st the effective date for the transfer of the First Battalion of the 21st Engineers (Aviation) to be transferred to MacDill Field for permanent station. Apparently this was to be a complete battalion less a cadre to be furnished the 42nd Engineers (GS).[37] These instructions were sent to the Commanding Officer of the 21st Battalion on the 31st of may, who enclosed them in a letter of inquiry to MacDill field.[38] The letter of inquiry from the Commandant of the Infantry School at Fort Benning asked for information about the date when the preparations would be completed to receive the Battalion. The date set by the authorities here was the 20th of June, 1940.

In accordance with these plans, the 21st Battalion of Aviation Engineers arrived at the Field on the 21st of June, 1940.[39] There were fifty men included in this organization led by Captain Lee B. Washbourne from Little Rock, Arkansas. These men were to form the nucleus for an organization that would include about 220 recruits, of which 119 were to come from the Tampa Area.[40]

After the 21st Engineers had been established on the Field and had even been assigned some work to do[41] and uniforms had finally been issued to the recruits[42] word was received that the organization was to be transferred to Langley Field without personnel and equipment, pending removal to permanent station at Fort Eustis, Virginia. The personnel and equipment which was not to accompany the transferred organization was to be absorbed by the 2nd Battalion of the 28th Engineers.[43] This transfer was to be made effective the 1st of July. The General Order implementing this change was published at MacDill Field on the 16th of July.[44] Apparently the transfer of the personnel of the 21st Engineers to the 28th Engineers was expected to increase the size of the units assigned to the 2nd to something like 20 officers and 500 men.[45] However the total strength of the four companies that made up the 2nd Battalion was only 337 men as of October 25, 1940.[46]

The work of these Engineering units, as has already been pointed out, was to construct certain Air Corps installations such as landing fields, bombing ranges, and other purely military installations that were not generally 1st to private contractors. Furthermore, they were to be trained so as to accomplish these missions in time of war and under fire. The training for the eventual discharge of this mission was of a most practical nature. Actual landing fields necessary to the expansion of the Air Corps were established as were bombing ranges and other installations. The way in which this work was accomplished was well described by the man who was in charge of their work, Colonel Tinker. In September of 1940 he wrote to General H. H. Arnold in the highest terms of phrase for these units. "The 2nd Battalion, 28th Engineers, which was organized here is living up to the reputation of the Engineers Corps", Colonel Tinker said. "I gave them one month to organize and get ready to work. The first task assigned them was the construction of a practice bombing range at MacDill field. In about three weeks from the time they started the construction, the 29th Bombardment Group was bombing on the range. Every task which I have given them has been carried out in a very workman-like fashion. I thought you might want to know this due to the fact that the assignment of Engineers to this type of duty is a new venture. I have nothing but the highest praise for their work".[47]

The 2nd Battalion of the 28th Engineers was composed of four companies. There was the Headquarters and Service Company under the command of 2nd Lieutenant Evans; Company A under the command of Captain Lee Washburn; Company B under the command of 1st Lieutenant Parker; and Company C under the command of 1st Lieutenant Pickard.

The other organizations are still to be accounted for in the records. These two units were the

Finance Department Detachment and a detachment of the 3rd Communications Squadron. The origin of these units have not yet been determined from the records, but both were here in June of 1940 and stayed on the base during the months under discussion. The authorized strength of the Finance Department Detachment was given as eleven and the 3rd Communications Squadron was authorized to have thirteen men.[48]

When the original plans for the units to be stationed at MacDill Field were drawn up, it was expected that the 221st reconnaissance Squadron would be sent from Langley Field with the 29th Bombardment Group.[49] However, the 21st was on patrol duty with the Navy and was temporarily stationed at Miami Beach. For that reason, the office of the Chief of the Air Corps informed Colonel Tinker that the Squadron would not be included in the movement from Langley Field. However, funds were earmarked for the transfer as soon as its patrol duty was terminated.[50] Nevertheless, the Commanding Officer of the Langley Field Air Base informed the Commanding Officer of the 21st Reconnaissance Squadron that Langley Field would cease to be the supply point for this organization after the 15th of May, 1940. for that reason all equipment, supplies, and personnel that had been loaned to the organization by Langley Field would have to be returned. Furthermore, requisitions would not be accepted or engine changes made after the 10th of May.

It isn't clear from the records just how the 21st was able to have its Base needs cared for during this period. However, in July the Headquarters of the General Headquarters Air Force requested the Commanding General of the 3rd Wing to submit a plan for its transfer to MacDill. The request did state that the Squadron would remain on detached service at Miami until further notice. This request was passed on to the Commanding Officer of MacDill field to accomplish. From the exchange of radios that took place upon Colonel tinker's receipt of this request, it would seem that neither Colonel Tinker nor the 3rd Wing were clear on the exact status of the 21st. "Status of the 21st will be sent you as it is determined."[51] Colonel Tinker submitted his plans which, in substance, recommended that the 21st Squadron should remain in the tent camp at Miami, which had been erected to house them until MacDill was ready for flying.[52] This recommendation was apparently well received by higher headquarters, for when the Adjutant General's Office instructed the Commanding General of the General Headquarters Air Force to issue the orders transferring the unit to MacDill Field on the 10th of October, it very specifically stated that "The squadron (is) to remain on temporary duty at Miami Florida." Nevertheless, its Base was MacDill Field and eventually it left Miami to take its residence there.

The assignment of the 21st Reconnaissance Squadron to MacDill Field, although on temporary duty at Miami Beach, completed the roster of the units that were assigned to Colonel Tinker's command up to the 1st of October, 1940. Only one other change remains to be discussed and that was more or less an administrative change rather than a change involving personnel shifts. This change re-designated the Base Headquarters and 27th Air Base Squadron as the 27th Air Base Group. The new group consisted of three squadrons; the Headquarters and Headquarters Squadron, the Air Base Squadron, and the Material Squadron. The change took place the 1st of September.[53] The reason back of this change was to divide the original Air Base Squadrons into units that accomplished the carious functions necessary for an Air Base. These new squadrons making up the Air Base Groups were assigned according to their function of caring for administration, Air Corps supply, or maintenance work. The Headquarters Squadron being charged with the administrative function, the Air Base Squadron, looking after the supply function, and the Material Squadron doing second echelon maintenance for the Base. To accomplish this change, the original personnel was divided according to the duties they had previously discharged, and assigned to the Squadron indicated to supervise those duties.

During the period in which these units were being assigned to MacDill Field, the growth was extremely rapid. From 828 men actually on the Base in May, when Colonel Tinker arrived to take command, the soldier population doubled in June, reaching 1749 men. In July the number of enlisted men on the Field was raised to 2166 men. This was higher than the figure originally set for the Field when all of its installations had been completed. The Army's expansion, and the Air Corps in particular, was proceeding so rapidly that MacDill Field had to accept this larger number before planes were able to land or take off from the landing strips that were gradually taking shape on the airdrome site. August reported practically the same number of men, there being 2133 that month. However, September showed another month of rapid increase, reaching 2527 men by the 26th day.

BIBLIOGRAPHY

1. Letter to Chief of Air Corps from Colonel C. L. Tinker, Air Base Headquarters, Barksdale Field, February 13, 1940. Subject: Movement of Detachment to MacDill Field, paragraph 1a, file 370.5.
2. Tampa Tribune, March 16, 1940.
3. History of Medical Department, Station Hospital, MacDill Field, Florida, April 1, 1940 to December 7, 1941.
4. SC #75, Air Base Headquarters, Langley Field, Va., March 29, 1940, paragraph 1.
5. Hospital Order #1, Station Hospital, MacDill Field, May 1, 1940.
6. AG 370.5 (4-19-40) E. Orders, April 17, 1940. To: Commanding General, 4th Corps Area, SO #95 Air Base Headquarters, Barksdale Field, Shreveport, Louisiana, April 27, 1940.
7. Letter: "Plan of Movement of the 29th Bomb Group (H) to MacDill Field, Tampa, Florida, Headquarters GHQ AF, Langley Field, Virginia, March 16, 1940. To: The Chief of the Air Corps, Washington, D. C., paragraph 3d.
8. History of Medical Department, Station Hospital, April 1 to December 7.
9. 370.5 Letter Colonel Tinker, AB Headquarters, Barksdale Field, February 13, 1940 to CAC, paragraph 5.
10. 726.1 Station Hospital, MacDill Field. Subject: Venereal Report. To: The Commanding Officer, AB Headquarters, MacDill Field.
11. History of 28th Air Base Squadron, appendix #1.
12. 726.1 Monthly Venereal Report, April 27, 1940. To: Commanding Officer, MacDill Field, Florida.
13. AG341 (5-16-40) E. AGO, May 16, 1940. Subject: Preparedness Requisition No. 1. To: Commanding General, 4th Corps Area.
14. SO #32, MacDill Field, May 27, 1940, st. seq.
15. SO #45 MacDill Field, June 12, 1940, paragraph 10.
16. Ibid., paragraph 9.
17. General Order #6, MacDill Field, June 11, 1940. Auth. Letter AG 320.2 (5-31-40) M (Retired) C-M, dated June 9, 1940. Subject: Activation of Signal Platoons (AB) to Commanding General, GHQ AF.
18. SO #122, MacDill Field, September 19, 1940. Authorized by GO #23, Headquarters GHQ AF Langley Field, September 11, 1940. Telegram M 5811 S, from Headquarters 3rd Wing, Barksdale Field, September 24, 1940.
19. 370.5 Memo to Base Headquarters, MacDill Field, August 22, 1940. Attention: Colonel Jacobs.

20. File 726.1 Monthly Venereal Report. To: The Commanding Officer, MacDill Field, dated 27 April 1940.
21. Letter Headquarters, 4th Corps Area, file 370.5 General, dated April 23, 1940. SO #95 AB Hq., Barksdale Field, April 27, 1940.
22. 370.5 General Headquarters 4th Corps Area, April 29, 1940. Subject: Specially qualified Quartermaster Corps Personnel for MacDill Field, Florida. To: Commanding Officers of all Posts, including exempted stations and offices, this Headquarters.
23. GO #5, Air Base Headquarters, MacDill Field, June 11, 1940.
24. GO #8, August 17, 1940, MacDill Field, Section I, paragraph 1, and Section II, paragraph 1.
25. File 370.5, WH 39 F. Radio from Commanding General, 3d Wing. To: Commanding Officer, MacDill Field, September 28, 1940.
26. SO #159, MacDill Field, November 6, 1940, paragraph 1.
27. File 726.1 Monthly Venereal Reports for months indicated; file 331.3, Memorandum from Air Base Headquarters to PX Officer, MacDill Field, dated 26 September, 1940. Subject: Authorized strength of Organization.
28. Ibid.
29. 370.5 WD AGO AG 370.5 (4-19-40) M-M, May 15, 1940. Subject: "Movement of Detachments, 10th Ordnance Company to MacDill, McChord, and Moffett Fields." To: Commanding General, GHQ AF, Langley Field, Virginia.
30. SO #119 Air Base Headquarters, Langley Field, May 20, 1940, paragraph 3.
31. SO #118, Barksdale Field, May 28, 1940.
32. AF 370.5 Commanding General, 3d Wing, September 19, 1940. Subject: "Movement of Cadre." To: Commanding General, 2nd Wing, GHQ, AF, Langley Field.
33. SO #32, MacDill Field, May 27, 1940.
34. SO #106, MacDill Field, August 31, 1940.
35. File 220.313 Detachment 3rd Weather Sq., AC, MacDill Field, September 16, 1940. Subject: Administration of Det. 3rd Weather Sq., AC. To: Commanding Officer, MacDill Field.
36. SO #125, MacDill field, September 23, 1940.
37. Letter AG 320.2 (5-20-40) M-C-M, AGO, May 25, 1940, paragraph 13.
38. 370.5 AGO May 31, 1940.
39. Tampa Tribune, June 22, 1940.
40. Ibid
41. Tampa Tribune, July 7, 1940, clearing the building and landscaping the grounds for the Army Service Club in Tampa.
42. Tampa Tribune, July 7, 1940.
43. AG 320.2 (6-28-40) M (Retired) M-C WD AGO, July 6, 1940, paragraph 5 and 6.
44. GO #7.
45. Tampa Tribune, July 13, 1940.
46. 726.1 Venereal Report, October 29, 1940.
47. 201 file, Tinker, C.L. Letter Colonel Tinker to General H. H. Arnold, September 3, 1940.

48. Memo: Air Base Headquarters, MacDill Field, 26 September 1940 to the PX Officer.
49. Tampa Tribune, March 8th and 10th 1940, 370.5 Letter Office of Chief of AC, April 4, 1940. Subject: Movement of troops to MacDill Field. To: Commanding Officer, MacDill Field, paragraph 4.
50. 370.5 Office of the Chief of Air Corps, May 1, 1940. Subject: Movement of the 21st Reconnaissance Squadron to MacDill Field.
51. 7 WVR JF 51WD, Radio Barksdale Field, August 8, 1940 to the Commanding Officer, MacDill Field.
52. 201 File, Tinker, C. L. Letter from Colonel Tinker to General Arnold, September 3, 1940.
53. AG 320.2 (6-12-40) M (Retired) M-C WD AGO August 22, 1940, Subject: Air Base Groups. To: Commanding Generals of Corps Areas and Commanding General, GHQ AF Langley Field, paragraphs 1 and 2.

CHAPTER VII

ATHLETICS, RECREATION AND THE PX

The enlisted men that were commanded by these officers found their life at MacDill Field quite different from that led at Langley Field in Virginia. Where Langley Field presented the comforts as well as the completeness necessary for efficient work found in a well established military installation, MacDill Field presented the discomforts and incompleteness generally associated with field service. The incompleteness of the Field was dramatically presented to these pioneers from Langley Field when they had to be transported several miles to Drew Field in order to do the work that they were trained to do. Two hundred men were detailed to go to Drew and live in tents for duty connected with the operations work of the Group. After spending half of the month on this duty, the detail would returned to the barracks at MacDill and another would go in its place for the rest of the month. While living at MacDill the enlisted men in the Twenty Ninth were used on fatigue details, which consisted of clearing work as well as the usual police work.[1] On the whole though, life was not too strenuous on the Base during these peace times. A usual day called for the enlisted men to answer for Reveille at 6:45 with breakfast call coming in at 7:15. They reported for duty at 8:00 and worked at the duty assigned them until 11:30 when recall was sounded. They reported for work after the noon meal at 1:00 again, and continued their work day until 4:30 in the afternoon, when recall brought them back to get ready for retreat. Two afternoons of the week were actually given them for recreation when they would try to catch fish, go swimming or simply lie around the barracks and write letters.[2]

Nights were definitely reserved for amusement and romance in Tampa; that is except for the unlucky individuals that were detailed for guard duty. The rest were usually pre-occupied with the sport that Tampans had taught them to call "jookin". This sport was an ancient one that probably came from Europe with the Spanish Colonists to Florida, and certainly entered the northern colonies by way of England. In short "jookin" was simply the Floridians name for the "pub-crawl". This might not have been the best way to amuse themselves, but it did give them an opportunity to meet the people of Tampa who were found to be most hospitable. Nevertheless, the amusements provided for the soldiers at MacDill Field serve to underline the essential lack of organized amusements for the peacetime Army enlisted men. This can hardly serve as an indication of indifference on the part of the people of Tampa, nor, for that matter of the officers in charge. One of the first speeches that Colonel Tinker made in Tampa called attention to this situation existing in general around Army camps. In that speech he called attention to the fact that recreation facilities were not provided by the government and the lack of them created one of the biggest problems to face army officers.[3] To meet this problem, Tampans built a club house, located at Tampa and Tyler streets, for the enlisted men. While this act testifies to the desires of the citizens of Tampa to do what they could for the enlisted men, the fact remains that the club was not as great a success as must have been hoped for when it was inaugurated. Some of the men did not even know that it existed[4], possibly because plans were not made for well worked-out programs.

This situation was aggravated by the fact that the Field was not completed. Athletic facilities were practically non-existent, and the only sports that were open to the men were those that required little beyond outdoor space, and not too much of that.[5] This situation plagued both the men and the officers alike and was the subject of much thought by those in command.[6] However, the will was there and an outdoor basketball court was set up as well as a soft ball diamond. In this latter sport the Base was able to put out a team that was sufficiently proficient to take the runner-up honors in the Tampa Soft Ball League that summer.

This lack of recreation was underlined by the absence of any sort of arrangements for the showing of motion pictures. Several requests for some means that would make it possible to provide movies for the men were sent to the Office of the Chief of Air Corps. Each time they were refused. One attempt was made to put movies on the field is worth mentioning.

In some fashion, Mr. F. L. Slig was granted permission in November 1940 to show motion pictures in a tent, he to provide the pictures and equipment. In order to do this, Mr. Alig approached the Atlanta distributors for bookings of current pictures. Knowing that the Army generally booked films for showing in Army camps through the War Department Motion Picture Service, the distributors referred the matter to the Headquarters of the Fourth Corps Area. This action resulted in a letter forbidding the future showing of motion pictures in that manner. This blocked the first real attempt to provide the men on the field with such entertainment. [5a]

The seriousness of the situation increased as the population of the Field increased and this was reflected in the venereal rate. More than three thousand men were housed on MacDill Field when the next attempt to get movies shown on the Field was made. At that time, the nearest theater was in Tampa, nine miles away, and it was felt that the emphasis should be placed on keeping the men in camp as far as possible. Colonel Tinker, on the strength of this assumption, wired the Adjutant General's Office, requesting permission for the Post Exchange (established by that time) to rent equipment and pictures and present them to the military personnel of the Field until such time as a War Department Theater was in operation on the Field.[6a] This request was denied for some reason, but the Adjutant General did leave the door open for showing of movies on the Field before a War Department Theater was erected. Apparently it was possible to get films and equipment from the United States Army Picture Service if some sort of space was available. For that reason it was suggested that information be supplied concerning available building facilities.[7]

Upon consideration it was decided that the Quartermaster Maintenance Warehouse would be the most suitable building that could be made available for the purpose. This information was sent to the Adjutant General's Office with the additional information that a theater could be completed in from three to five months. The warehouse itself could be made ready for use by December 1940, and would seat approximately one thousand persons.[8]

The Adjutant General, with customary caution, approved the selection of the warehouse with the stipulation that the space would not be required by the Quartermaster Corps. He also sent a check for six hundred dollars ($600) to pay for building materials necessary to remodel the building and install seats. The Engineer of the United States Army Motion Picture Service, the Adjutant General's letter reported, was to report to MacDill Field to supervise the work of converting the section of the warehouse that had been set aside to a temporary theatre.[9]

The first men arriving on the Field were faced with the problem of making purchases of minor items, such as cigarettes, candy and items of personal clothing, on a field located some nine miles from the nearest shopping district. To alleviate this condition the officers of the Twenty-seventh Air Base Squadron took one of the day rooms assigned to that squadron and turned it into a Post Exchange for the use of the men in the organization. Likewise a restaurant concession was given to a Mr. Barrows, who sold beer and soft drinks with his sandwiches.[10] This business was located in a temporary building to the northwest of the present location of the Fire and Guard House, and was the scene of the nightly gathering of a large part of the enlisted men of the Post. The only difficulty with the organization arose when the Twenty-ninth Group was moved to the Field. Then it was found that the day room of the 27th Squadron was too small to care for the crowds that thronged it every night. In fact the 27th complained that they were unable to make their own purchases after surrendering their day room. As a result of the difficulty Lieutenant John R. Kane, Adjutant of the 27th, issued a memorandum on 5 June 1940 to the effect that only personnel of the Base Headquarters and the 27th Air Base Squadron Could be served at the day room.[11]

Whether this development caused the subsequent events or not, the next morning at 8:30 A.M. a meeting of representative officers of all organizations at MacDill Field was called to consider the question of the organization of a Post Exchange for the entire field. This meeting was attended by Lt. Colonel M. C. Grow, who acted as president, Major Louis Cansler of the Det. 5th Sig. Ser. Co., Major J. F. Greene of the 238th Sep. Q.M. Co., Co.L, Major C. T. Skow, Post Exchange Officer, Major C. E. Conner, Base Headquarters and 27th Air Borne Squadron, Major H. P. Rush of the 6th Bomb Squadron, Major W. G. Bryte, Headquarters and Headquarters Squadron, 29th Bomb Group, Captain J. A. Samford, 43rd Bomb Squadron and Captain G. R. Barnes, 3rd Platoon, 333rd Ordinance Company.

The results of this meeting were to establish a Post Exchange for the Base and the general policies designed to govern it. It was adopted as a general policy governing the Post Exchange that it should operate without granting concessions, but keep all of its services under the direct supervision of the Exchange. It was decided that there should be a general merchandise section that include tobacco products and bus, street car and theatre tickets. Likewise a beer and soft drinks section should be maintained, as well as a tailor shop and a shoe repair shop. Such facilities as laundry, barber shop, grocery, soda fountain and restaurant were not included in the prospectus for the Post Exchange. [12] The meeting did not forget certain of the amenities that were to prove popular with the post. One of these was the appointment of a committee to inquire into the feasibility of erecting an opened screened pavilion for the purpose of a beer garden.

It was recognized that a Post Exchange would also have to be erected at Drew Field for the use of the men that were stationed there for duty with the combat crew. It was suggested by the meeting to the committee appointed to consider the advisability of the Post Exchange at Drew that it might be either a Twenty-Ninth Bomb Group Canteen or a branch of the Post Exchange at MacDill Field. [13] This matter was settled by Colonel Tinker in a memorandum to the President of the Post Exchange Council. This memorandum laid down the policy that "any sub-exchange will be a branch of the main exchange." In this way, any future difficulties that might have arisen from having independent organizations carrying on the same functions under the direct command of the field were avoided. Furthermore, it spelled the doom to such organizations as had been established by the 27th AB Squadron's exchange. Thus, responsibility and authority was centralized in the hands of one Post Exchange Officer for the field. [14]

The capital for the Post Exchange venture was provided by the officers and enlisted men in the units housed on the Field under the provisions of paragraph 13 AR 210-65 that were effective in 1940. Under these provisions the Post Exchange sold shares of stock to all persons eligible to receive them and wished to participate in the revenues of the organization. Those eligible were the officers and enlisted men stationed on the Field. Usually the squadrons bought the shares for the number of men enrolled in their organization.[15] The money used by the Squadron for this purpose came from the Squadron funds, which then received the profits from the organization for the use of the personnel of the squadron owning the stock. In addition to these organizations purchases of stock, individual officers stationed on the Field could likewise purchase one share of stock and receive the benefits of purchasing in the Post Exchange and sharing in the profits so derived according to their shares.

The management of the Post Exchange was placed in the hands of a Post Exchange Officer who was responsible to the Base Commander and the Post Exchange Council. The Post Exchange Council acted as the real governing body, authorizing expansion of facilities, [16] personnel and local policy in general. [17] The Commanding Officer confined his control of the Exchange principally to formally approving application from Squadrons for membership, requiring that Army Regulation and directives were observed and laying down the broad lines of policy under which it was to be conducted.

BIBLIOGRAPHY

1. Based on interview with CWO Richard Keller, Base Det., MacDill Field, Tampa, Florida.
2. Tampa Tribune, 16 March 1940 and Interview, CWO Richard C. Keller.
3. Tampa Tribune, 25 may 1940.
4. Interview with CWO Keller.
5. Letter of Information, File No. 004.52. Subject: Motion Picture Shows, For the Commanding General, MacDill Field. TO: the Adjutant General Washington, D.C., dated 7 November 1940.
6. Ibid.
7. Radiograms (October 17 and 23, 1940) Adams to MacDill Field.
8. Radiogram (October 29, 1940) tinker to Adjutant General, Washington, D.C.
9. Letter (November 15, 1940) 1st Lt., R. G. Conklin to AG, Washington, D.C. 2nd Ind. from C. G., MacDill Field to C.G., 3rd Wing, GHQ Air Force, Tampa, Florida. (December 7, 1940) on original letter (December 5, 1940) Headquarters GHQ Air Force, Langley Field, Va.
10. Letter (November 15, 1940) 1st Lt. R. G. Conklin to AG, Washington, D.C.
11. Letter (December 7, 1940) Adjutant General, Washington, D.C., to C.G., MacDill Field, Tampa, Florida.
12. File No. 331.3PX, Letter for information, Subject: Post Exchange, from Major Charles T. Skow, Post Exchange Officer, to C. O. MacDill Field, 8 July 1940).
13. File No. 331.3 PX, Memorandum, 4 June 1940.
14. File No. 331.3 PX, Minutes of a Meeting called to organize a Post Exchange, Headquarters AB, MacDill Field, 5 June 1940.
15. Ibid.
16. File No. 331.3 PX, Memorandum to President of Post Exchange Council by order of Col. Tinker, 18 July 1940.
17. File No. 331.3 PX, 6 June 1940, Subject: Application for Membership in Post Exchange, to Commanding Officer, MacDill field from Captain John A. Samford, Commanding Officer, 52nd Bomb Squadron.
18. File No. 313.3 PX. Letter 19 July 1940, Subject: Dry Cleaning and Laundry Agency, from Post Exchange Officer to Commanding Officer, MacDill Field. Same File, Subject: Purchase of Post Exchange Shares, Commanding Officer Base Headquarters and 27th AB Sqn. to Commanding Officer, MacDill Field, dated 13 June 1940.
19. File No. 331.3 PX, Letter 22 November 1940, Subject: Recommendations for the Post Exchange, from major O. L. Blan, Acting President to Commanding General, MacDill field.

CHAPTER VIII

VENEREAL DISEASES

It would be possible to draw up convincing arguments to prove that there was a close connection between the dearth of social organizations to satisfy the normal desire for amusements of the young men of army age and the tragic development of the venereal disease rate at MacDill Field during the first summer and early fall of the military occupation of the Base.

During the first month and a half of the military occupancy of MacDill Field there were no cases of venereal disease reported by the Station Dispensary or Station Hospital.[1] This record was made while the Base was enlarging its population from forty-three[2] to one hundred and fifty three enlisted men.[3] On the 29th of April the first case came to the attention of the medical authorities, followed by another on the third of May, and a third on the seventh of May. Two more cases developed in the last week of May, being discovered on the 27th and 29th days, to bring the consolidated report for the period ending 31 May to five cases. This gave an actual rate of sixty-three per thousand per annum. All of these reported cases concerned enlisted men in the Headquarters 27th Air Base Squadron. This was the oldest squadron on the Field, having sent a detachment that arrived on the 11th of March and the rest of the squadron on the 22nd of April. Thus the record credited against the Base rightfully belonged to that squadron and the rate for five week period ending May 31, 1940.[4] The seriousness of this development of the venereal rate is apparent when contrasted with the actual rate (and the MacDill Field rate was an actual and not general one) of thirty-seven per thousand for the whole corps area.[5]

This report, as has been pointed out, was actually the record of one squadron as all of the cases but two were reported before the arrival of the Twenty-Ninth Bomb Group, although their strength was counted in the total strength of Colonel Tinker's command in arriving at their rate. As a matter of fact none of these incoming squadrons reported any cases for May. However, the June reports show that three of the four squadrons reported one man each as having developed a venereal disease. Two of the three Quartermaster Units also reported cases, the QM Company No. 238 reporting two cases. There was also one case each reported from the 3rd Platoon of the 333rd Ordnance Company and the 1st Battalion Engineers. The Base Headquarters and 27th Air Base Group reported three cases, the largest number reported. Thus of twenty-one units on the Base, eight reported that one or more of their personnel had developed some form of venereal disease. Two of these organizations, the Base Headquarters and 27th AB Group and the QM Company 238 had excessive rates. The total number of cases reported for June was eleven. The strength of

Colonel Tinker's command had then reached 1794 and the rate was computed at seventy-nine per thousand per annum.

This high actual rate fell to seventy-two per thousand per annum in July, but the number of cases rose to fifteen. Of these, three cases were contracted outside the control of the military authority of the Post, thus reducing the number of cases to twelve. The general rate was ninety per thousand. Thus there was a net increase of only one case to be counted in the actual rating over June although the strength of the command had risen to two thousand, one hundred and sixty-six. The units reporting cases were the Base Headquarters and 27th Air Base Squadron, two of the four squadrons in the twenty-ninth Bomb Group, one company of the four in the 28th Engineers, two of the three quartermaster units and the medical department detachment, a total of seven out of nineteen units on the Field.

August reported the peak in the number of venereal cases reported. There were nineteen cases reported among the two thousand, one hundred and thirteen men under Colonel Tinker's command. Of these nineteen cases four were not chargeable to the Base. This was a rise to ninety-two in the actual rate per thousand and one hundred and sixteen in the general rate.[6] Twelve of the twenty-two units on the field reported cases included in the total. Of these the Base Headquarters and 27th Air Base Squadron reported the largest number of cases - five. All four of the squadrons in the twenty-ninth Bomb Group reported cases as did two of the four units in the 28th Engineers and two of the six QM units. The Medical Department Detachment, the 3rd Platoon of the 33rd Ordnance Company, and the Casual Detachment also reported cases.

Fortunately this dangerously excessive rate for the Field declined in September. In spite of the fact that the total strength for the field increased to two thousand, five hundred and twenty-seven during that month, the number of venereal cases dropped to fourteen. Of these, nine were not chargeable to the Post.[7] Only ten units reported cases at this time in contrast to the twenty-two for the month previous. This was the first time, according to available data, that the Field dropped below the actual rate of the IVth corps Area, the actual rate of MacDill Field being twenty-five and the actual rate of the Corps Area being forty-eight.[8] However, the general rate remained somewhat higher than the Corps Area's area, the Field having a general rate of seventy-nine and the Corps Area having a general rate of sixty-one.

This blot on MacDill Field's record caused a great deal of concern to the responsible officers and all others interested in its welfare. The Commanding Officers of the units with excessive rates were promptly queried as to the underlying causes of the prevalence of the disease. The conclusions of the unit commanders varied a great deal. A good many seemed to think that the movement of the troops into a new territory had affected the more settled tendencies to be found at an established post. In other words they felt that there was a definite tendency to explore new territory when the men were off duty.[9] Possibly the underlying idea back of this suggestion lay in the enthusiasm with which Tampa greeted their new soldier population, giving them the idea that they were privileged to act as they pleased. More practically, some of the officers complained of the prevalence of infected women in the Tampa Area, particularly in Ybor City. How many infected women that were in the area was unknown, but these officers thought that there were a large number of them.[10]

In line with these suggestions, the youth and inexperience of the enlisted men, the bulk of whom were hardly more than recruits, was advanced as a reason.[11] The only difficulty with this suggestion is that it fails to satisfactorily answer the question raised by the great disparity between the MacDill Field rate and that average of the IV Corps Area. Presumably the other parts in the Area were faced with the same problem of youth as MacDill Field as a result of the expansion of the Army.

Suggestions that the men did not have sufficient knowledge of Army prophylactics and that the administration of prophylaxis was at fault for certain reasons did have practical effect upon the action that followed. Equipment that had been lacking because of preoccupation with the building program was now obtained and methods of handling prophylactics were revised to meet the problem posed by the adverse conditions existing in the Tampa Area.

Lectures on sex morality were, of course, given in accordance with Army Regulations. But some of the Officers felt the need for more advice than the routine prescribed by regulation and gave talks, both in private and to their units, as frequently as possible. [12] These lectures stressed not only the morality of the questions, but also emphasized Army Prophylaxis.

One of the most practical steps taken to meet the problem was to provide a supply of individual prophylactic kits designed to sell for about fifteen cents. Colonel Young ordered the Surgeon to submit recommendations for such kits on the 29th of April, the very day that the first case of venereal disease was detected on the Field and the first week that the entire Base Headquarters and 27th Air Base Squadron was located here. These kits, when they were procured, were placed on sale in the squadron exchange. Apparently, the sale of these articles were not properly handled, for it later developed that they had to be purchased from the women employees. [13] Under such circumstances the kits were not purchased by the men. This situation was corrected by placing the sales in the hands of the Charge of Quarters who was instructed to sell them at all hours of the day and night. [14]

Major Witcher, the Commanding Officer of the Quartermaster units on the Field, took a more direct approach to the problem. This officer had insisted from the very first that the difficulties that the Field were experiencing with venereal disease was due to the youth and inexperience of the recruits that were filling up the ranks of the Army. Whether he complied the prevalence of venereal disease in Tampa with his suggestion of the underlying cause is not recorded. At any rate, he decided to go after the matter himself. He personally gave the morality lecture and then bought prophylactic kits with company funds. These kits were then issued to the men when they left for Tampa. [15] Whether these measures taken by Major Witcher were of any value in reducing the incidence of venereal disease or not, the fact remains that the months succeeding the establishments of the Quartermaster units the rate per thousand dropped sharply. From an actual rate of 6,723 per thousand in June 1940 the rate declined to 672 in July, 62 in August and no cases at all in September. After pioneering in the fashion, other commanding officers followed Major Witcher's example. In July the Medical Department Detachment inaugurated a similar system.[16] In August the Base Headquarters and 17th Air Base Squadron adopted the same procedure, [17] as did Company "E" of the 28th Engineers. [18] In September, the Base Headquarters was able to write the 4th Corps Area that prophylaxis kits were being bought by the organizations on the base for free issue to the enlisted men.[19]

One other factor that played a large part in reducing the incidence of venereal disease on the field was the establishment of prophylactic stations in Tampa. This project was initiated on the 16th of May, 1940, at a conference between Lieutenant Nethery, Medical Corps Res., and Mayor Chancey. As a result of this meeting, Lt. Colonel Young asked the Base Surgeon, Lt. Colonel Malcolm C. Grow, to have a conference with Dr. McEachern to arrange for the establishment of the prophylactic station.[20] At this meeting it was decided that the eventual location of the station be in the enlisted men's club in downtown Tampa. However, the difficulties of getting materials and the desire to get the post established caused them to decide to make use of the room in the building belonging to the Health Department of the City of Tampa at the corner of Scott and Tampa streets.[21] The arrangements made it possible to open the station on the 31st of May[22] and on the 11th of June. Two enlisted men were assigned to duty as attendants, working two twelve hour shifts each day.[23]

The arrival in September of the first colored troops to be stationed at MacDill Field required that facilities similar to those set up for the white troops be set up. This apparently was done in the latter part of October.[24] The site selected for this second station was at 1003 1/2 Scott Street in a small room adjoining and connecting with the offices of Dr. J. A. White, a negro physician. This site was contributed by Dr. White without charge and was reported to be satisfactory in every way save one - it was hard to find. The station was in the second story at the building on Scott Street and the outside stairway was unmarked so that finding its location was difficult,[25] although Dr. White's contribution was appreciated, and it was felt that he should be reimbursed. Since the Quartermaster could not provide funds for such a building it was decided to move the Station to the Public Health Building as soon as facilities at the Enlisted Men's Club could be provided for the white troops.[26]

BIBLIOGRAPHY

1. File No. 726.1 Venereal Reports (weekly) dated 23rd and 30th March, 5th, 19th, 27th April 1940.
2. File No. 726.1 Monthly Venereal Report dated 4 April 1940.
3. File No. 726.1 Consolidated Monthly Report of Venereal Disease for IVth Corps Area dated 24 May 1940.
4. File No. 726.1 Venereal Report dated May 31, 1940.
5. File No. 726.1 Consolidated Monthly Report of Venereal Disease for the 10th Corps Area dated 24 June 1940.
6. File No. 726.1 Venereal Report MacDill for the Period August 1 to 30, 1940. The rate given there is in error according to their formula.
7. File No. 726.1 Venereal report, MacDill Field for the period ending 27 September 1940.
8. File No. 726.1 consolidated Venereal Report, Fourth Corps Area, September, 1940.
9. File No. 726.1 Monthly Venereal Report for MacDill Field, 31 May 1940, 2nd Ind. Base Headquarters and 27th Air Base Squadron to Commanding Officer, MacDill Field, 10 June 1940.
10. File No. 726.1 Monthly Venereal Report for MacDill Field, 31 May 1940, 2nd Ind. Base Headquarters and 27th Air Base Squadron to Commanding Officer, MacDill Field, 10 June 1940. Same File: Monthly Venereal Report 26 July 1940, 2nd Ind. Det. Med. Dept. to Commanding Officer, MacDill Field, 5 August 1940, paragraph 1.
11. File No. 726.1 Monthly Venereal Report for MacDill Field, 1 July 1940. 3rd Ind. Commanding Officer, MacDill Field, to Commanding General IV Corps Area, Atlanta, Georgia. Same File and Report, 2nd Ind., Hq QM Company no. 238 (Sep) MacDill field to Commanding Officer, MacDill field, 10 July 1940.
12. File No. 726.1 Monthly Venereal Report, 1 July 1940, 2nd Ind., Base Headquarters and 27th Air Base Sq. to Commanding Officer, MacDill field, 18 July 1940. Same Report: 2nd Ind. Hq. QM Company No. 238 (Sep) to Commanding Officer, MacDill field, 10 July 1940.
13. File No. 726.1 Monthly Report for 26 July 1940, 2nd Ind. Base Hq. and 27th Ab Sqn. to Commanding Officer, 10 July 1940, Paragraph 1.
14. Ibid.
15. File No. 726.1 Venereal Report for MacDill Field, 1 july 1940, 2nd Ind., Hq. QM company (Sep), MacDill Field, 10 July 1940 to Commanding Officer, MacDill Field.
16. File No. 726.1, Venereal Report, 26 July 1940, 2nd Ind., Det. Med. Dept., 5 August 1940 to Commanding Officer, Hq. Air Base, MacDill Field.

17. File No. 726.1, Venereal Report, 26 July 1940, 2nd Ind., Base Hq. and 27th air Base Sq., 10 August 1940, to Commanding Officer, MacDill Field.
18. File No. 726.1 Venereal Report, 26 July 1940, 2nd Ind., Co. "E" of the 28th Engineers, 6 August 1940, to Commanding Officer, Base Headquarters, MacDill Field.
19. File No. 726.1 Venereal Reprot, 27 September 1940, 2nd Ind., Air Base Hq., MacDill field, 4 October 1940, to Commanding Genereal, 4th Corps Area.
20. File no. 726.1, Memo for Col. Grow, Subject: Prophylactic Station, 17 may 1940, from Colonel H. H. young.
21. File No. 726.1, Above Memo, 1st Ind., Station Hospital to Colonel Young, 25 may 1940.
22. File No. 726.1, Monthly Venereal Report, 31 May 1940, 3rd Ind., A.B. Hq., MacDill Field, 11 June 1940, to Commanding General, 4th Corps Area.
23. S.O. No. 47, AB Hq., MacDill Field, 15 June 1940.
24. File No. 726.1, Monthly Venereal Report for MacDill, 29 October 1940, 3rd Ind., Co. "H" 31st Quartermaster Regiment (trk), MacDill Field, 12 November 1940, to Commanding General, MacDill Field.
25. File No. 726.1, Station hospital, MacDill Field, Subject: Special Sanitary Prophylactic Stations in the City of Tampa, to the Base Surgeon, Station hospital, MacDill Field.
26. Ibid. Penciled note by Col. H. H. Young under 1st Ind., also paragraph No. 3 of 2nd Ind., Air Base Hq., MacDill Field, 27 December 1940, to The Surgeon, Base Hospital.

CHAPTER IX

CONSTRUCTION THROUGH 1941

The task of adding new fields and expanding old fields throughout the country was one of great magnitude. Particularly needed for the various construction programs was the closest measure of co-operation between different organizations. The chief organizations and their relationship to each other were as follows:

"The Corps of Engineers is charged with the direction of all construction at all Air Corps Stations (Panama excepted). The Quartermaster Corps is charged with the maintenance of buildings and facilities when completed and turned over by the Engineer Corps. The initiation and preparation of plans and general layout requirements up to the point of their approval by the War Department is a responsibility of the Chief of the Air Corps. The Chief of Engineers assists by furnishing the required cost data and engineering advice. Construction responsibilities are decentralized by the Chief of Engineers to Division Engineers and in turn to District Engineers. Project Engineers, serving as assistants to District Engineers, and are in immediate charge of construction projects. Air Corps responsibilities are largely decentralized to Air Force, Training Center, and Maintenance Command Commander, and, in turn to the Commanding Officer of the field concerned."[1]

It was particularly important that there should be the closest co-operation between District and Project Engineers and the Commanding Officer of the station. It was pointed out that they should be virtually in daily communication with each other. To facilitate construction, they were empowered to work out minor changes together.[2]

During 1940, various delays and mistakes were made in carrying out the building program at MacDill Field. Aware of this, and believing that it was wise to invite frank criticism of the policy so far followed, the Commanding Officer (25 November) asked various unit officers on the field to express in writing their complaints.[3] The answers to this inquiry are interesting.

Lt. Colonel Vincent Meloy, Commanding Officer of the 29th Bombardment Group, submitted the following recommendations to be followed in planning a new Air Base: Roads and utilities should be constructed first. Recreational facilities for troops should be made available at earliest possible date. Provision should be made for emergency heat in barracks and tents, for cooling and refrigeration in kitchens, and for adequate fire protection which should keep pace with expansion. Operating, administration and supply buildings should be constructed early. Adequate maintenance funds should be promoted from the beginning.[4]

Captain G. R. Barnes, Base Ordnance Officer, submitted a report on particular difficulties encountered incident to the activation of MacDill Field. Time and trouble would have been saved, he wrote, if a more permanent type of road system had been constructed initially. Because of the rapidly expanding number of troops provisions for barracks, mess halls, service warehouses and shops had not kept pace with the needs. Adequate supplies of tools and equipment had been difficult to obtain. Funds for the construction of an ammunition magazine and bombing ranges had been delayed or were inadequate.[5]

The failure to provide at an early date sufficient buildings for religious welfare and recreational programs was stressed by 1st Lt. Willard G. Davis, Chaplain, who pointed out the importance of such installations to morale.[6]

Despite this criticism, much of which undoubtedly proved helpful, considerable progress was made in the construction of installations during the year 1940. The two largest projects were the building of hangars and runways.

Plans for three hangars, to be built at an estimated cost of $1,200,000 were received from Washington on 15 June 1940. One of these, the so-called "Base Hangar", was to be a combination shop and plane storage building, with office and warehouse spaces two stories high at each side. Its dimensions were 338 feet wide by 274 feet deep. The other two hangars were to be used chiefly for plane storage. Each was to be 274 by 279 feet. All three hangars were to constructed of steel and concrete and have arched roofs. Sliding metal doors were to provide an aperture 200 feet wide. The plans were drawn up by the Arch Roof Construction Company, New York City.[7]

Work on these three hangars had been complete by December, 1940, and the hangars were already in use. Two additional hangars were in the process of construction and were scheduled for completion by 15 April 1941. Upon completion of all five hangars it was estimated that MacDill Field would have sufficient hangar space. [8]

In June, 1940, the Army announced that it would receive bids on the construction of three runways to be constructed at MacDill Field. It was estimated that the total cost would be approximately $700,000. Plans called for asphalt runways 5,000 feet long and 150 feet wide.[9]

The contrast for the runways was awarded July 9, 1940, to the Ebersback Construction Company, Tampa, Florida, the lowest bidder. The Ebersback Company agreed to complete the work in one hundred and forty days at a cost of $745,832.[10]

Actual laying of the runways began on 14 August, 1940. Work proceeded rapidly and on 27 September Colonel Tinker was able to announce that the concrete work on runway No. 1 would be completed the next day. It was expected that by 10 October the laying of concrete on the other two runways would be finished. If the present speed could be maintained, said Colonel Tinker, operations might begin on the 1st of December.[11]

The hangars and runways were the largest single building projects for the second half of 1940, but a score of other activities were going on concurrently. Hundreds of soldiers and civilians were engaged in the work of clearing ground, landscaping, remodeling and building. Crews from the 21st Engineers, under the direction of Lt. V. B. Culberson, were occupied with putting the grounds into shape and beautifying the field. The 5th Signal Service Company was installing a temporary telephone system. Barracks, mess halls, supply buildings, day rooms, a wing to the

Administration building, and a temporary Headquarters Building were among the projects under construction. As early as 7 July 1940 direct allotments and WPA appropriations totaled more than $6.000.000.[12]

A building project particularly important for the morale of enlisted men was the construction of housing units for married personnel of the first three grades. The question of quarters for married noncommissioned officers at MacDill Field was first raised in April, 1940, when a questionnaire was circulated to determine if there existed in Tampa and its surroundings a sufficient number of suitable houses and apartments. The increasing need for rentals of this type was made apparent by the questionnaire.

GUARD HOUSE & FIRE STATION, PHOTO LAB.
& WAREHOUSES, MACDILL FIELD, FLA.
SECRET

(0115-7771-21R)(1-3-41-11:14A)(12-1500) BUILDING AREA, MACDILL FIELD, FLA.

(G344-21R)(1-3-41) OFFICERS QUARTERS, MACDILL FIELD, FLA.

(G338-21RX1-3-41) FIRE STATION AND GUARDHOUSE, MACDILL FIELD, FLA.

HOSPITAL AREA, MACDILL FIELD, FLA.

HANGAR & WAREHOUSE AREA, MACDILL FIELD, FLA.

In the summer of 1940 a low-cost housing project was undertaken by the Housing Committee of Tampa. It was hoped that some of the units in this project would be available for non-commissioned officers.[13]

On MacDill Field itself work was started on six units designed for non-commissioned officers. The construction of these quarters was completed in August, and the following month the units were assigned to six non-commissioned officers.[14]

Because the real problem of housing facilities had not been met, Colonel Tinker, Commanding Officer at MacDill Field wrote (6 August 1940) to the Adjutant General in Washington, requesting that the War Department recommend to the Federal Housing Authority that up to five hundred housing units be built near MacDill Field for the use of married non-commissioned officers.[15] Action was soon forthcoming, and the Tampa Tribune announced a Federal Housing plan to erect low-cost units near MacDill Field.

The actual contract for the construction of housing units at Gadsden Park was made on 12 December 1940 between the Federal Works Agency and the Paul Smith Construction Company of Tampa, Florida. It called for the construction of three hundred housing units (101 buildings) on a Cost-Plus-A-Fixed-Fee contract. The cost of the project was estimated at approximately $816,000 exclusive of the contractor's fixed fee of $40,000. Building operations were to begin within a week. [17]

Men were moving to MacDill Field in large numbers during 1940, and despite the numerous added installations, the building program did not keep pace with the growing personnel. In September, therefore, Base Headquarters at MacDill Field submitted a list of the temporary construction requirements needed to complete a housing plan for the then authorized strength of 516 officers and 5,883 enlisted men. In addition to hospital installations the plans called for the following:

Item	Capacity	Size Feet	Units Required	Total Cost
Adm. Bldg.	44 Clerks	25 x 106	4	$20,800
Barracks	63 Men	30 x 80	52	390,000
Day Rooms (Colored Troops)	125	25 x 72	1	2,500
Day Rooms	250	25 x 72	14	49,000
AC Gasoline and Oil Storage				103,000
Mess, EM (Colored)	170	25 x 87	1	4,800
Mess, EM	250	25 x 108	14	75,600
Mess, Officers	250	25 x 108	2	10,800
Operations Bldg.	44 Clerks	25 x 108		15,600
Post Exchange	3,000	37 x 99	1	8,500
Quarters, Officers	40	29 x 130	6	78,000

Motor Repair Shop Q.M.	4 Stalls	37 x 84	1	7,000
Recreation Bldg.		37 x 99	1	9,600
Sqn. Supply Warehouses		25 x 51	13	32,500
Telephone Installations				5,000
Theatre	1,038		1	55,000
Warehouses, AC		60 x 153	1	14,000
Warehouses, QM		60 x 153	1	14,000
Warehouses, CMS		60 x 153	1	14,000
Interior Roads				75,000
Concrete Roads				82,500
Garage				2,850
Walks				15,000
Dredging	(No Figures)			
			Total	$1,422,300[18]

Plans for hospital buildings were submitted at the same time, and on 12 November a large scale construction program began on the hospital buildings. These hospital facilities, with the exception of one infirmary and one dental clinic, were located at the former Quarantine Station, approximately two miles south of the main area on MacDill Field. Several buildings formerly occupied by the Quarantine Service were to be used in addition to the new installations. Work progressed rapidly, and the entire hospital group was completed by 30 June 1941.[19]

The buildings included the following: One (1) administration building at a cost of $11,000, quarters and mess for Medical officers at a cost of $8,850, one (1) Quarters and mess for nurses, costing $11,950, two (2) buildings to house nurses at a cost of $6,350 each, one (1) storehouse at $9,000, another at $15,000, a Hospital Mess Hall and kitchen at $21,000, one (1) Dental Clinic at $13,300, a heating plant built at a cost of $30,000, two (2) Barracks costing $8,250 each, and Infirmary at $8,500, a day room costing $3,500, six (6) medical and surgical wards built at a cost of $69,396.[20]

During the first part of 1941 a large group of WPA workers were engaged in landscaping, minor construction and excavation on MacDill Field. Materials and equipment for these workers were furnished by the War Department. Although the WPA did not construct buildings, erect runways, or participate in the creation of projects for which contracts were awarded, it contributed much towards putting the field into shape. On 15 July 1941 a total of eight hundred and twenty-seven WPA workers were employed at MacDill. their work consisted of filling operations throughout the building area, grading and drainage of land, placing and finishing lime rock, pouring concrete sidewalks and curbs, planting grass plots on the air field, laying pipe for sewers, minor finishing on several buildings, pumping sand ashore to fill in low ground, setting forms, pouring casings for electrical conduits, road construction, backfilling and making manholes.[21]

Special arrangements were made to allow WPA workers to work a forty-eight hour week instead of the thirty hour week which was customary. The number of WPA workers increased later in 1941, and in September as many as 1,400 were employed at MacDill Field.[22]

One of the best summaries of building activities on MacDill field is contained in a report July 18, 1941. It shows the installations already completed and the stage of completion for buildings under construction.

More important contracts:

Approved	Structure	Percent Completed
06/06/40	Photographic Lab	100
03/19/40	Non-Commissioned Quarters	100
06/18/40	Fire and Guard House	100
07/05/40	4 Warehouses	100
10/03/40	5 Single Field Officers' Quarters	100
09/11/40	Runways	100
09/28/40	Air Corps Gas Fueling System	100
10/04/40	Hangars	98.8
09/28/40	Water Tank (500,000 gallons)	100
10/04/40	Electrical Dist and Street Lighting	100
09/28/40	Night Lighting System	99
11/23/40	Radio Transmitter Building	100
11/28/40	Plumbing and Heating, 96 Buildings	100
12/31/40	Night Lighting System	100
02/01/41	Plumbing and Heating, 96 Bldgs.	100
02/13/41	Dredging, 75,000 cubic yards	100
01/18/41	Theater	57
01/23/41	Radio Beacon Range Building	97.8
02/10/41	Plumbing and Heating, Hospital Group	100
03/15/41	Apron Additions	100[23]

The status of construction of the major groups at MacDill field on 30 June 1941 was:

Administration and Housing.. 86% Complete
Medical Corps Installations.. 100% Complete
Technical .... 100% Complete
Permanent Construction .... 54% Complete
Complete Air Field.. 64% Complete

According to the 18 July 1941 report the following buildings and facilities had been completed and turned over to the control of the Commanding Officer:

(a) Temporary Type Construction:

Type	No.
Barracks, 63 men	73
Mess Buildings, 250 men	18
Mess Buildings, 117 men	3
AC Storehouses	13
Warehouses	8
Adm. Buildings	12
Parachute Building	1
Inflamable Storage	1
Day Rooms	12
Officers' Mess	2
Officers' Quarters	5
Recreation Building	1
Post Exchange	1
Operations Building	4

(b) Permanent Construction:

Type	No.
Non-Com. Officers' Qts.	3
Paint, Oil Storehouse	1
Signal and Ord. Warehouse	1
QM Warehouses	2
QM Warehouses and Commissary	1
Fire and Guardhouse	1
Field Officers' Qts.	5
Steel Water Tank	1
Radio Transmitter Building	1
R.R. Spur	1
Concrete Runways and Aprons	3
Gas Meter House	1
AC Oil Storage Sys.	1
Additional Concrete Aprons	2
AC Gasoline Fueling Sys.	1
Motor Pool and QM Gas Stations	3
Radio Beacon Range Building	1
AC Hangars	2[25]

Generally, the Chief of the Air Corps in Washington approved the plans submitted for additional buildings but there was one notable instance when he refused, for the time being, to allow additional facilities to be constructed. On 16 June, 1941 the Commanding General of

MacDill Field sent a request to higher Headquarters, asking that two additional warehouses of 9,000 square feet capacity be constructed. This additional space was urgently needed, he said, to take care of Air Corps supplies on hand and en route to the base.[25a] In reply the Chief of the Air Corps in Washington, D.C., asked for a list of all buildings being used as warehouses on MacDill Field.[26] This inquiry revealed that there were in July 1941 the following warehouses on the field: Four with a total of 32,000 square feet, assigned to Air Corps Supply; five with a total of 38,700 square feet, allotted to the Quartermaster Corps,; one warehouse with 5,000 square feet for the Engineering Department; one warehouse with 4,000 square feet used by 100% Priority Units for storage; two Ordinance Warehouses with a total of 8,200 square feet, one Chemical Warfare Warehouse of 2,000 square feet; one warehouse used by the 810th Engineers of 7,000 square feet; and one Signal Corps Warehouse of 7,200 square feet.[27]

After reviewing this list, the Chief of the Air Corps rejected the request for additional warehouse space. He pointed out that warehouse space was apportioned according to the strength of a base. Warehouses for Quartermaster supplies were allotted on a basis of 7 1/2 square feet. Therefore, MacDill Field already had approximately 20,000 square feet of warehouse space over and above the allowance under existing policy.[28]

Because MacDill Field was located on Tampa Bay, various advantages could be obtained by utilizing this body of water. Before boats of deep draft could be put into service, however, it was necessary to dredge a channel through the Bay and provide docking facilities at MacDill Field. A survey of this project had been completed on 9 April 1941 by the District Engineer at Jacksonville, Florida, and plans were sent through channels to high authorities. Various proposals and changes were suggested. For instance, it was recommended that the dredged material might be used as a fill for the parade ground and other low areas on MacDill Field, thereby saving the expense of hauling filling material a great distance.[29]

Authorization for the project was finally made on 27 August 1941 with an allotment of $243,986 to cover the cost of dredging and constructing wharf age facilities.[30]

Bids were opened 27 October 1941 for constructing bulkhead, wharves, and two piers, and on November 10th for dredging operations. In addition to dredging a channel nine feet deep, the contractor was to dredge a basin which would allow boats at the dock to turn.[31]

It was planned to berth the following boats at the MacDill Dock: Three seagoing vessel boats, length 83 1/2 feet, draft 4 1/4 feet, beam 15 feet, 7 inches; two shallow draft boats; two picket boats; one armored target boat, 179 feet long, 9 feet draft, and 32 feet beam; one utility boat. Other craft were to be added in future years.[32]

During the fall of 1941 various recreational buildings were completed and opened to soldier personnel of MacDill Field. First on the list came the theater. Movies had at first been shown on the field in a large tent, then part of a Quartermaster warehouse had been taken over, and finally the whole building. But these had never been more than temporary arrangements and plans for a theater to seat 1,038 persons were approved as early as 18 January 1941.[33]

Construction of the theater was completed in time for a grand opening on Sunday, 21 September 1941. The new building was modern in every detail. One entrance was through a glass enclosed lobby. Inside there were indirect lights, rows of seats built on an incline, an orchestra pit, and a twenty by forty stage. Heavy insulation and ventilating fans provided protection against the hot weather. The projection room was fireproof, with concrete floor and ceiling and asbestos covered sidewalls. Ample emergency exits were provided. [34]

Special ceremonies marked the opening of the new theater. A short, dedicatory address was made by Colonel Harry H. Young, the MacDill Field Commander. The Tampa Elk's Band was there to provide music. Soldiers, eager to see the newest recreational building, filled every seat in the $70,000 Theater - complete with the latest type projectors and sound equipment. The first movie, starring Marlene Dietrich, Edward G. Robinson, and George Raft, was appropriately entitled "Manpower".[35]

A few weeks later MacDill Field celebrated the opening of the Service Club. This building, which cost $45,500 to construct, had, besides a cafeteria, a large dance floor measuring sixty by eighty feet, lounges, offices, a spacious balcony, a screened porch, and a large room on the second floor where the library was to be temporarily housed. The Club opened Saturday evening 11 October 1941, with the band of the University of Tampa and the dance orchestra of Manuel Sanchez. Girls for the opening night dance were provided by Defense Mothers of Tampa and St. Petersburg. There was a floor show with a soldier cast. Colonel Young made a dedicating speech which was broadcast. [36]

With the completion of the Service Club, a large room was set aside for a library of 5,000 books. These were selected from various fields to suit the varied reading interests of soldiers. Men were encouraged to drop in, smoking was permitted, and informality was the rule. In charge of the library from its initiation was Miss Kathleen Fletcher. [37]

A little later in the fall the two chapels on MacDill Field were completed and formally opened. Contracts for the construction of these buildings had been awarded 23 June 1941 and construction began in August. The Chapels built at a cost of $21,000 each were similar to the hundreds of other chapels on Army posts. The exterior was modeled after a New England Meeting House. Accommodating four hundred worshippers, each chapel was so arranged that Protestant, Catholic, and Jewish Services could be held in them. The interior was marked by a fitting simplicity of design. Services were held in the two chapels on Sunday, November 2, although dedication ceremonies did not take place until Thursday, November 6. Speakers at this ceremony were Colonel Young and Chaplain Edmund Friffin of the 3rd Air Force. Benediction was given by Chaplains Murray E. Love and William T. Gaynor. [38]

The year 1941 closed with plans already formulated for constructing an area to house colored troops. Late in the summer of 1941, the Chief of the Air Corps had asked all Air Force Bases to submit by November 1, 1941 a list of new construction requirements with items which were to have first priority indicated. At MacDill Field it was felt that a building project to house colored personnel was the one most urgent. Plans were submitted, therefore, for sixty-six buildings to be erected in an area near the Port Tampa Gate, MacDill Field. [39]

The following buildings were called for: 28 barracks, 10 mess halls, 11 supply rooms, 10 day rooms, a theatre, an infirmary, a post exchange, a recreation building, quarters for officers, an officers' mess building, and an administration building. These installations, it was estimated, would be constructed at a total cost of $470,100. [40]

Other items on the priority list were additional buildings for the hospital area, including 10 wards. Large sums were asked for the construction of utilities and for the installation of streets, sidewalks and curbs. The total cost of all these items, including buildings for the colored area, was estimated at $1,277,397.41

BIBLIOGRAPHY

1. Ltr., 8 May 1941, War Dept. Office of Chief of Air Corps to Commanding Officers of all Air Corps activities.
2. Ibid
3. Memo, 26 Nov 1940, Headquarters, 29th Bombardment Group, MacDill Field, to Commanding General.
4. Ibid
5. Ltr., 26 Nov 1940, Base Ordnance Officer, MacDill Field to Base Executive.
6. Ltr., 26 Nov 1940, Base Chaplain, MacDill Field to Commanding Officer.
7. Tampa Tribune 16 June 1940.
8. Ltr., 4 December 1941, Capt. S. H. Killgore, Adj., MacDill field, to Chief, Air Service Command, Wright Field, Dayton, Ohio.
9. Tampa Tribune 29 June 1941.
10. Tampa Tribune 27 Sept 1940.
11. Tampa Tribune 10 July 1940.
12. Tampa Tribune 7 July 1940.
13. Ltr., 1 July 1940, to Col. Tinker from G. D. Curtis, Secretary, Tampa Chamber of Commerce.
14. Special Order No. 107, 1 Sept 1940, issued by order of Col. tinker.
15. Ltr., 6 Aug 1940, from Col. Tinker to AG, Washington, D. D.
16. Tampa Tribune, 21 Sept 1940.
17. Ltr., 12 Dec 1940, to CO, MacDill Field, from W. E. Reynolds, Commissioner of Public Works, Washington, D.C.
18. Temporary Construction Requirements, MacDill field, 9 Sept 1940.
19. Construction Report on MacDill Field, 18 July 1941.
20. Ibid and Ltr., 26 May 1941, U.S. Engineer Office, MacDill Field to Commanding General, MacDill Field.
21. Construction Report on MacDill field, 18 July 1941.
22. Ltr., 19 Sept 1941, Engineer Corps, MacDill Field, to Commanding Officer.
23. Construction Report on MacDill field, 18 July 1941.
24. Ibid.
25. Ibid.
26. Lt., 16 June 1941, General Tinker to Commanding General, 3rd Air Force, Tampa, Fla.
27. Op. Cit, 3rd Ind., 8 July 1941, War Dept., Chief of Air Corps to Commanding Officer, MacDill Field.
28. Op. Cit, 6th Ind., 22 July 1941, Hdqs., MacDill Field to Commanding General, 3rd Air Force, Tampa, Fla.

29. Op. cit, 9th Ind., 5 Aug 1941, Office of Chief of Air Corps, to commanding Officer, macDill field.
30. Ltr., 10 July 1941, from Lt. Col. Frank M. Paul to Gen. Tinker, MacDill field.
31. 17th Ind., 27 Aug 1941, Office Corps of Engineers to Division Engineers, Richmond, Va., on original Ltr., 9 April 1941, from Office of Engineer Corps.
32. 1st Ind., 28 Oct 1941, Project Engineer, MacDill Field, to Commanding Officer, MacDill, on Ltr., 20 Oct. 1941, Base Hdqs., MacDill Field, to Project Engineer.
33. Ltr., 7 Aug 1941, U.S. Engineer Officer, MacDill Field, to Commanding Officer.
34. Construction Report on MacDill Field, 18 July 1941.
35. Flyleaf, 5 Sept 1941.
36. Flyleaf, 19 Sept and 26 Sept 1941.
37. Flyleaf, 10 and 17 Oct 1941.
38. Flyleaf, 10 Oct 1941.
39. Construction Report on MacDill Field, 18 July 1941. Flyleaf, 31 Oct and 7 Nov 1941.
40. Ltr., 13 Oct 1941, AB Hdqs., MacDill Field to Project Engineer.
41. Op. cit., 1st Ind., 22 Oct 1941, U.S. Engineer Office, MacDill Field to C.O. and enclosure.
42. Ibid.

CHAPTER X

GENERAL TINKER LEAVES MACDILL

On October 3, 1940, Colonel Tinker received a telegram notifying him that the President had sent his name to congress appointing him temporary Brigadier General of the Army of the United States. This high honor was accepted by Congress and made effective as of October 1.This advance to the grade of general officer came to General Tinker shortly before his 53rd birthday. [1] As Brigadier General, General Tinker continued in his assignment as Commanding Officer of MacDill Field Air Base until the following January.

The change in duty for General Tinker was his assignment to be the Commanding General of the 3rd Bombardment Wing, General Headquarters Air Force, which he received the 10th of January, 1941.[2] This War Department order assigned General Tinker to an organization that had only recently arrived at MacDill Field. Formerly the Headquarters and Headquarters Squadron of the 3rd Wing, General Headquarters Air Force, it had been redesignated the 3rd Bombardment Wing on the 3rd of December, 1940 while at MacDill Field where it had arrived the 2nd of October, 1940.[3]

The new orders reassigning General Tinker officially relieved him of duty as Commanding Officer of MacDill Base before assigning him to the higher echelon, and he was to report to the headquarters of the General Headquarters Air Force at Langley Field for instructions by letter.[4] This General Tinker did on the 11th of January, indicating in his letter that he had received previous instructions from the General Headquarters Air Force to the effect that he would continue as Commanding General of MacDill Field as well take over the command of the 3rd Wing until such time as the Wing moved to Drew Field, which was apparently being contemplated as the future domicile of that organization.

This arrangement was permissible, as General Tinker pointed out, under the provisions of Army Regulations 210-10, which allowed a Post Commander to be at the same time the commander of a tactical unit, with the provision that the details of Post Commander to be left to the Post Executive officer.[5]

This arrangement was apparently satisfactory to the higher headquarters for it was confirmed by a telegram from the 3rd Wing, General Headquarters Air Force on the 16th of January.[6] The administrative organization, under this arrangement, provided General tinker with two staffs that were responsible to him and for which he was responsible for policy. Each staff carried on its duties independently although those duties were laid down for them by General Tinker. The base staff, under the immediate direction of Colonel H. H. Young, still continued to be the housekeeping unit, providing the training facilities necessary for the programs devised by the tactical organizations, and maintaining the buildings and constructing new ones to aid toward that overall end to the mission of the Base. The staff of the 3rd Bomber Wing continued to look after the training of the bombardment groups that flew heavy bombers and requiring that those groups properly maintain their technical equipment issued for training purposes. The great advantage of the arrangement from the administrative point of view was that the problems that involved the relationships of both staffs could be decided upon by the officer with authority over both groups. If the 3rd Bomber wing Staff made demands upon the Base Staff for equipment and facilities that were contrary to Base policies, their plan had to go to the officer that was responsible for that policy. On the other hand, if the Base Staff refused facilities or equipment which the tactical organization was entitled to have, they could be ordered to take the desired action by the officer that was responsible for the proper functioning of the program of the tactical group. The great handicap to this arrangement lie in the fact that the 3rd Bomber Wing was in charge of the training of units on Fields other than MacDill Field. This might lead to too great preoccupation with the welfare of one field if the commanding general did not exercise the most extreme caution. There is every reason to believe that General Tinker did exercise the caution and judgment to make the arrangement a success, but that weakness remained inherent in the organization that might lead to difficulties under a less apt leader.

This situation was changed in August of 1941 after General Tinker had relinquished his command of the Base and the Wing. Brigadier General Follett Bradley succeeded General Tinker on the 13th of August under the same arrangements that were permitted by the Army Regulations that had served for General Tinker.[7] Then the regulations were changed in that respect a few days after General Bradley assumed command. The new change made any officer ineligible to the Commanding Officer of the Base regardless of seniority, that was "assigned to an element of an Air Force other than an Air Base headquarters or Air Base Squadron."[5] It has already been pointed out that General Tinker had been first relieved of his duties as commanding officer of the Base when he was made commanding officer of the 3rd Wing, and he merely continued to act as commanding officer of the Base under instructions from the General Headquarters Air Force. Actually, General Bradley was assigned to 3rd Wing, and as such he was not eligible to be the Base Commander. Consequently, after only eight days of duty as Commander, General Bradley relinquished command[8] and Colonel Young took his place. Thus Colonel Young assumed the leadership of the Field for the second time in the short span of its history on the 21st of August.[9]

The relinquishment of the command of the 3rd Bomber Wing and the Base by General Tinker, removed that colorful figure from the direction of the Field, but not from the affections of the men that he commanded. It was a sad group that met to say hail and farewell to their commander at the Columbia Restaurant in Ybor City on the 20th of August. Not only were the men who had served him sad to see the General depart, but he himself probably regretted the turn of fortunes that required his change of station. But the change had to be, for the Office of the

Chief of Air Corps had need of his ability in other places. In fact, only his bad health prevented from going to a new station earlier.

During most of 1941 General Tinker had been in bad health, probably as a result of overwork and his responsibilities of his office. For some time he had been suffering from myalgia distress, particularly involving the muscles of the neck, dorsal spine, and shoulder girdle. The condition became chronic, and in July he was forced to be confined to bed. After making a physical examination and taking laboratory tests, the Medical Department recommended that General Tinker be transferred to the Army and Navy General Hospital at Hot Springs, Arkansas. It was hoped that the warm baths and physic therapy facilities would have a beneficial effect upon the myalgia.[10]

The orders assigning General Tinker to the Hot Springs General Hospital arrived at the field on the 17th of July, 1941 from the Fourth Corps Area Headquarters. Two days after their arrival orders from Washington arrived, ordering him to sail from Charleston, South Carolina for Panama.[11] Naturally these orders were turned over to the Third Air Force Headquarters where the advice would be forwarded to Washington of General Tinker's hospitalization.[12] During this period of General Tinker's hospitalization, Colonel Young assumed temporary command of the Base. In the middle of August, General Tinker was relieved of his command and attached to the Third Air Force in order to permit him to undergo the treatment prescribed at Hot Springs.[13] It was at this time that General Bradley assumed command of the Base.

"FOR EVERY FLIGHT:—A SUCCESSFUL MISSION, AND A SAFE RETURN!"

Thousands See Army's New MacDill Field Dedicated

—Times Staff Photos by Sandy Gandy

In the speaker's stand at the formal dedication of MacDill field yesterday were (left to right) Maj. Gen. Barton K. Yount, commanding the 3rd Air Force; Mrs. Leslie MacDill, widow of the Army colonel for whom the new southeastern air base is named; Congressman J. Hardin Peterson; Chairman Fred Ball of the Hillsborough county commission; Lt. Cmdr. Clarence F. Edge, commanding the United States Coast Guard air station, St. Petersburg; Brig. Gen. Clarence Tinker, commanding the Third Wing; Harry Playford, St. Petersburg aviation liaison officer; Brig. Gen. Herbert A. Darque, representing Maj. Gen. Henry H. Arnold, chief of the air corps; United States Senator C. O. Andrews and United States Senator Claude Pepper (speaking).

General Tinker's cure proceeded favorably during the summer and he was ready to return to Florida in October. On the 17th of that month the Washington Headquarters ordered him to take a medical examination.[14] Apparently his illness had not affected him physically for he passed the examination which made him eligible for promotion.[15] This promotion was confirmed on the 20th of January, 1942 and General Tinker was moved up to the temporary rank of Major General[16] -- a fitting climax to a long and successful career in the Army.

Shortly before his promotion, December 16th to be exact, General Tinker was ordered to Hamilton, California.[17] From there he was sent to the Hawaiian Department to take charge of that Air Force, and it was while he was commander of the American Air Force in Hawaii that he met his death in the Battle of Midway, the first American General to die in combat in the present war. Word of his death was sent to MacDill Field that owed so much to his leadership by Lieutenant General Delos C. Emmons, one of the men who had actively participated in the establishment of the Field and who shared with others the responsibility for the selection of General Tinker as the officer to lead the Base in its opening days. The notice that General Emmons sent was terse as all such tragic messages are. It read: "Major General Clarence L. Tinker, AC, 0-32S2, member of combat crew failed to return to operating base from an offensive bombing mission at sea on 7 June 1942, and is now being carried as missing in action."[18]

The death of General Tinker closed a chapter in the history of MacDill Field, for his life, from 1939 onward, in many ways symbolized the development of MacDill Field. His advance from the grade of colonel to the grade of a major general represented a great honor for the man. Likewise, and even more startling, was the rise of MacDill Field from a stretch of Florida wilderness to one of the finest air bases in America. This rise was bound up with and to a large extent was the result of the administration of General Tinker and the staff from which he evoked the greatest of loyalty and cooperation -- the mark of leadership. For this reason, the history of MacDill Field to the opening of this, the greatest war in history, is largely the biography of General Tinker.

The ferry boat "Gen. Clarence L Tinker",
heads to MacDill Field with servicemen aboard.
Note the landmark water tower in front of the ferry
and the rounded tops of the hangers just to the left.

REFERENCES

1. Telegram (Oct. 3, 1940) Adams, Washington, D.C. to Tinker, MacDill.
2. Telegram (Jan. 10, 1941) Adams, Washington, D.C. to Tinker, MacDill.
3. 3rd Air Force Files.
4. Telegram of Jan. 10, 1941.
5. Letter (Jan 11, 1941) Tinker to Commanding General, General Headquarters Air Force, Langley Field.
6. Telegram (Jan 16, 1941) Easterbrook to Commanding General, MacDill Field.
7. GO #13 August 13, 1941, MacDill.
8. GP #14 August 21, 1941, MacDill.
9. GO #15 August 21, 1941, MacDill.
10. Medical History of General Tinker (July 16, 1941) Capt. C. M. Serou, M.C.
11. Telegram (July 17, 1941) Hq. 4th Corps Area, Atlanta Georgia, to Commanding General, MacDill.
12. Telegram (July 18, 1941) Adams to Tinker, MacDill Field.
13. War Dept., Special Orders No. 193, (Aug 19, 1941).
14. Hq., 3rd Air Force, Tampa, Florida, Special Orders No. 149 (August 14, 1941)
15. Letter (October 17, 1941) Letter Adjutant General's Office, Washington, D.C., to Commanding Officer, MacDill Field.
16. War Department, Washington D.C. Special Orders No. 17 (Jan 20 1942)
17. Air Base Hq., MacDill Field to Commanding General, 4th Corps Area, Atlanta, Ga.
18. Telegram (June 14, 1942) Emmons to Commanding General, MacDill Field.

AIR BASE HEADQUARTERS
Barksdale Field

Special Orders
No. 54

Shreveport, Louisiana
March 7, 1940

EXTRACT

1. Pursuant to authority contained in Letter, WD, AGO, file AG 370.5, 27th Base Squadron (2-20-40) M-C-M, subject: Movement of Air Base Detachment to MacDill Field, Florida, the following named officer and enlisted men, 27th Air Base Sq (S) will proceed by rail on or about March 9, 1940 to MacDill Field, Florida, for permanent station. Travel by privately owned conveyance is authorized for the enlisted men listed in Par. 1b, under the provisions of Par. 1i, AR 35-4820, for such enlisted men as are not required to accompany the troops, as authorized by Par. 2d, above mentioned letter:

a. 1st Lieut. Robert B McClellan, Air-Res

Sgt Clarence E. James, 6110506
Corp James B Beard, 6264091
PFC Sp6cl Bernard B. Bragg, 6663482
PFC Sp4cl Kenneth D. Ellison, 6664770
PFC Sp6cl Aubrey A. Cason, 6925131
PFC Edward A. Ladner, 6392674
PFC Sp3cl Harry A. Monroe, 6921236
PFC Sp5cl Irvin H. Reynolds, 6925118
PFC Sp5cl Paul R. Wiggins, 6925089
PVT Bruce Jones, 6968411
PVT Sp6cl Leonard Randall, 6966966
PVT Sp6cl Charles L. Taylor, 6967128

Sgt Howard Bruce, 6225349
Corp Lynwood L. Bright, 6306237
PFC Sp6cl George L. Cockrell, 6925228
PFC Sp5cl Robert L. Green, 6799596
PFC Woodrow W. Kelley, 6399106
PFC Sp5cl Louis A Linton, 6383962
PFC Sp4cl William A. McKinney, 6418118
PFC Jacob B. Rexer, 6920981
PVT George R. Dukes, Jr., 6972621
PVT Sp6cl Everett W. Wall, 6964965
PVT Sp3cl Camp F. Tinnin, 6265054
PVT John I. Keasler, 7001275

b.

Tech Sgt Joseph O. Schreck, 6313358
St Sgt Johnny J. J. Pegram, 6232847
Sgt William J. Hunter, 6533784
PFC AM2cl Russell E. Chappell, 6830871
PFC AM2cl Seals G. Edwards, 6242691

PFC Sp1cl Ola E. Ferguson, 6730114
PFC Sp6cl George A. Javor, 6274909
PFC AM2cl Frank G. Little, 6637917
PFC AM2cl Thomas E. Moore, 6264935
PFC Edward C. Nelson, 6733226

St Sgt Curtis N. Eckerty, 6637917
St Sgt John D. Skinner, 6369143
Sgt George C. O'Dell, 6717699
PFC Sp6cl Raymond R. Cleek, 6398946
PFC Sp6cl Christopher C. Ferguson, 6397120
PFC Sp5cl James W. Hendrix, 6393874
PFC Sp6cl Ottis B. Jones, 6344436
PFC Sp2cl Gayland W. Magness, 6275890
PFC Sp2cl Floyd E. Morrison, 6265017
PFC AM2cl Arthur L. Vaughan, 6265035

PFC AM2cl Fred A. Wilson, 6256528
Pvt Sp6cl Bryce D. McCray, 6275104
Pvt John C. Robider, 6972618
PFC Sp5cl Ocie N. Tekell, 6925050
Pvt QM2cl Leo N. O'Connor, 6833870
Pvt Sp3cl Barney C. Simmons, 6265057

c. The Quartermaster Corps will furnish the necessary rail transportation.

d. Such available equipment as is shown for peace in Column Three of Tables of Basic Allowances, plus trunk lockers, will accompany the unit. Individual clothing and equipment will be taken by each enlisted man. No ammunition will be taken.

e. A delay not to exceed five (5) days is authorized the enlisted men listed in Par. 1 b above.

S.O. No. 54, B.F., March 7, 1940, (Cont'd) (Extract)

PARAGRAPH 1, CONT'D.

f. The travel directed above is necessary in the military service and payment when made is chargeable to procurement authorities listed below:

Travel of the Army: FD 2437 P 1-0620, P 50-0623, P 80-0600, P 82-0600 A 0410-0 (For travel of the Air Corps officer and enlisted men by rail; for travel of dependents of the officer and enlisted men of the first three grades.)

Army Transportation - Rail: QM 1620 P 72-0110, P 72-0284, P 72-1378, P 54-0700 P 61-0700, P 59-0700 A 0525-0 "D" (For packing and crating and shipping organizational equipment and impedimenta and authorized allowances of baggage of the officer and enlisted men of the first four grades; and for tolls and ferriages en route).

g. The Quartermaster and Finance Officers to whom expense account in connection with this order are submitted for payment will submit a detailed report, by purpose numbers under each procurement authority to the Commanding Officer, Barksdale Field, Louisiana, as soon as practicable after the above mentioned movement has been completed in accordance with Par. 13, Ar 35-1040.

By order of Colonel BRERETON:

/s/ E. W. Hampton
E. W. HAMPTON,
2nd Lt., Air Corps,
Assistant Adjutant.

OFFICIAL:
/s/ E. W. Hampton
E. W. HAMPTON,
2nd Lt., Air Corps,
Assistant Adjutant.

Distribution:
25 - Finance Officer, Barksdale Field, La
50 - Transportation Clerk, QMC
6 - Each Enlisted man Par. 1 b
100 - 27th Air Base Sq (S)
15 - 1st Lt McClellan
16 - T/Sgt Schreck

CERTIFIED A TRUE COPY:

JOHN R. JONES,
2nd Lt., Air Corps.

AIR BASE HEADQUARTERS
Office of the Commanding Officer
MACDILL FIELD

Tampa, Florida
April 7, 1941

SUBJECT: Administrative Reserve Officers

TO: Commanding General, Third Air Force, National Guard Force, Tampa, Florida

1. According to the latest information at these headquarters, MacDill Field should have (or is to accumulate) a pool of Administrative Officers for distribution as follows:

MacDill Field	49
Augusta, Ga	12
West Palm Beach, Fla.	24
Baton Rouge, La.	11
New Orleans, La.	12
	108

This is a reduction of 23 from the number shown on quota chart, G-1 Section, dated December 6, 1940, enclosed with letter, your headquarters. Subject: Chart Covering Quotas of Administrative Officers GHQ Air Force, date January 4, 1941. The quota of 108 is verbal but believed to be correct.

2. Today, MacDill Field has 65 Administrative Officers present for duty, four of these being assigned to 53rd Pursuit Group (I) and one to 29th Air Base Group, units scheduled to transfer to Tallahassee and Charlotte, respectively, at any time, which would leave a balance of 60 Administrative Officers against a quota of 108.

3. To date, MacDill Field has lost (or will lose, including Tallahassee and Charlotte) 35 officers to units other than those listed in paragraph 1 and no replacements have been received.

4. Ten of the 65 Administrative Reserve Officers now at MacDill Field have applied for and passed the physical examination for air craft observer. When, as and if ordered, these officers will also require replacement.

5. By letter to your headquarters, dated March 28, 1941. Subject: Personnel Overhead - Tent Camp, MacDill Field, these headquarters requested additional personnel of 21 officers and 52 enlisted men to operate the semi-permanent tent camp established here at MacDill. Commanding General, Third Air Force, Tampa, Fla. - Administrative Reserve Officers.

6. The administrative overhead of officers is daily becoming more acute. In order that the officers referred to in paragraph 1 may have all training possible prior to transfer to permanent stations, that MacDill Field acquire its full complement of officers and that the tent camp be amply supplied with officers and enlisted men, it is request that suitable officers be ordered to MacDill Field as soon as practicable, and authority be granted to establish the detachment of enlisted men for the tent camp.

/s/C. L. Tinker

C.L. TINKER
Brigadier General,
Commanding.

This is a TRUE COPY

/s/ John R. Jones
John R. Jones
2nd Lt., Air Corps,
Historical Officer.

Subject: Administrative Reserve Officers.

210.31 1st Ind. (L-3)

HEADQUARTERS 3rd AIR FORCE, Tampa, Florida, April 11, 1941

TO: Commanding General, MacDill Field, Florida.

1. Many changes have been necessary since the original quota and allocation of reserve officers was announced. MacDill Field has been practically the only source of this type personnel available for movement to new stations, or for school details, as the total at Savannah Air Base has never exceeded fifty (50), and the requirements for both stations are almost identical.

2. It appears quite certain at this time that your present balance will not be diminished, and that those previously intended for Baton Rouge and New Orleans will be furnished from non-Air Force stations.

3. This headquarters has been advised that the allotment of administrative reserves to Air Force stations has been doubled, and that procurement will become effective in the very near future. Your difficult situation in the training and losing of this type personnel is fully understood, and every possible effort will be made to curtail your future losses. However, as additional officers are received it may still become necessary to ask for recommendations on partially trained personnel, on order to assist commanding officers at the several new stations now being activated.

4. In regard to your paragraph 5, and to letter referred to dated March 28th, higher headquarters has announced that additional personnel for such purposes is not available. Until this situation can be corrected it will be necessary for you to use available officer personnel, and enlisted men by detail.

By command of Major General YOUNT:

/s/ C. A. Easterbrook
C. A. Easterbrook
Lieut. Colonel, A. G. D.,
Adjutant General

This is a TRUE COPY
/s/ JOHN R. JONES
JOHN R. JONES
2nd Lt., Air corps,
Historical Officer

AIR BASE HEADQUARTERS
MITCHEL FIELD

Special Orders Hampstead, L.I., N.Y.,
Number 88 April 15, 1940

1. The following named enlisted men, 27th Air Base Squadron, accompanied by Lieutenant Colonel Douglas Johnston, Air Corps, and First Lieutenant Lucio E. Gatto, Medical Corps Reserve, on temporary duty as officers-in-charge of Troop Train, and Private lcl Marvin Clark, R-1015172, Base headquarters and 2nd Air Base Squadron (Single) GHQ Air Force, as Cook, pursuant to instructions contained in War Department radiogram to Commanding Officer, Mitchel Field, N.Y. dated April 15, 1940, and instructions contained in War Department letter, file AG 370.5 (4-4-40)M-M, subject: "Movement of Base Headquarters and 27th Air Base Squadron to MacDill Field, Florida:, to Commanding General, GHQ Air Force, Langley Field, Va., dated April 11, 1940, will proceed by rail at the proper time, from Mitchel Field, N.Y., to MacDill Field, Tampa, Florida, reporting upon arrival thereat to the Commanding Officer thereof for duty with their proper organization:

ROUTING NUMBER 5323

Pvt Raymond R. Acla, 6982097
Pvt Everett V. Albin, 6981243
Pvt Walter R. Anderson, 6981412
Pvt James A. Baccash, 6981699
Pvt Oliver P. Barker, 6903178
Pvt Henry L. Benedetto, 6981435
Pvt Joseph E. Bollent, 6982428
Pvt Napoleon N. Bonaparte, 6981251
Pvt Richard G. Bouck, 6982033
Pvt Harry D. Bourdo, 6981392
Pvt John A. Boyle, 6980819
Pvt Richard P. Bronson, 6982091
Pvt Donald M. Brooks, 6977968
Pvt Harris E. Buchner, 6981419
Pvt John Burger, 6977929
Pvt Charles A. Burgess, 6845693
Pvt Pascal H. Burke, Jr., 6981367
Pvt George W. Card, 6980355
Pvt Michael Casper, 6146977
Pvt Clarence J. Chappell, Jr, 6976531
Pvt Martin F. Clark, 6902837
Pvt Leonard E. Eisenhauer, 6983505
Pvt Frederick L. Elliott, Jr., 6978446
Pvt William E. Ellwell, 6977182
Pvt George C. Emrick, Jr., 6977223
Pvt Robert E. Farr, 6982085
Pvt Charles K. Ferguson, 6981420
Pvt Orlando Ferraina, 6982429
Pvt Joseph B. Ferraioli, 6979326
Pvt Frank E. Filock, 6982415
Pvt John E. Fitzsimmons, 6872596
Pvt George H. Fort, Jr., 6978416
Pvt Charles E. Fowler, 6982071
Pvt John J. Galvin, 6903631
Pvt Joseph F. Gangarossa, 6982176
Pvt Lawrence P. Gately, Jr., 6980843
Pvt Ernest V. Gelinas, 6147462
Pvt Frank V. Giordani, 6981876
Pvt Ralph Gordon, 6981327
Pvt Murray Grossman, 6981421
Pvt Robert S. Gutkin, 6981296
Pvt Michael Halik, 6982456

Pvt Edwin C. Clothier, 6978299
Pvt Ernest A. Cole, 6977733
Pvt Thomas B. Connery, 6977925
Pvt Robert D. Coons, 6981447
Pvt Fortunato G. DeCecilia, 6982056
Pvt Joseph C. Diana, 6902909
Pvt Daniel J. DiGiore, 6982069
Pvt Rudolph J. Dokoupil, 6979053
Pvt Walter A. Johnson, 6981453
Pvt Donald R. Judge, 6982098
Pvt Walter F. Judge, 6982084
Pvt Emil J. Kaluza, 6983513
Pvt John Karasik, 6979071
Pvt Eugene J. Karlick, 6978575
Pvt Bernard Kaufman, 6982424
Pvt Edward E. Keefe, Jr., 6981416
Pvt Frederick J. Knox, 6976977
Pvt Warren F. Lefkowitz, 6978460
Pvt John J. Lentz, 6981325
Pvt Nicholas Leva, 6981797
Pvt Louis LevenCrown, 6981373
Pvt Edward F. Lindley, 6977588
Pvt Edmund F. Lynn, 6885584
Pvt James R. McCarthy, 6980515
Pvt William A. McLeron, 6708616
Pvt Henry J. Malicki, 6983516
Pvt Michael G. Malinario, 6980884
Pvt George C. Mazalook, 6983523
Pvt Mike Melfa, 6978581
Pvt William H. Momberger, 6982229
Pvt Leroy N. Moore, 6978609
Pvt Douglas F. Morris, 6983501
Pvt William J. O'Connell, 6716725
Pvt George H. Ogilsbie, 6976715
Pvt Clement N. Olsen, 6901082
Pvt William O'Mahoney, 6129230
Pvt Walter A. O'Neill, 6973859
Pvt Ralph W. Pace, 6981463
Pvt Francis J. Heron, 6979748
Pvt Howard L. Hoffman, 6981526
Pvt Raymond E. Holcomb, Jr., 6976882
Pvt James P. Horton, 6980849
Pvt Richard A. Hoyt, 6980356
Pvt Henry L. Hutchinson, 6978304
Pvt George W. Jackman, 6980098
Pvt Maxillian Jerozal, 6983511
Pvt Curtis H. Pratt, 6980348
Pvt Pasquale Ricillo, 6978321
Pvt Mathew B. Rowe, 6907126
Pvt Robert B. Rugar, 6982096
Pvt Charles R. Ruslikas, 6904843
Pvt John L. Ryan, 6978608
Pvt Edgar J. Scott, 6902954
Pvt William A. Shafer, 6902168
Pvt John J. Shea, 6974285
Pvt Henry R. Shubert, 6976172
Pvt Norman Sigel, 6875269
Pvt Keith W. Smith, 6982231
Pvt Carl Sokolitsky, 6981283
Pvt Claude J. Southern, 6880291
Pvt Jack R. Sowers, 6850033
Pvt Edward J. Stafanski, 6940114
Pvt Floyd B. Stanford, 6979669
Pvt Glenn E. Starkweather, 6980357
Pvt Willis A. Steifel, 6982177
Pvt John S. Strelecki, 6982421
Pvt Henry J. Terranova, 6982416
Pvt John K. Thompson, 6980570
Pvt Thomas E. Towner, 6904827
Pvt Benjamin A. Valentine, 6977978
Pvt Angelo A. Varone, 6982413
Pvt John R. Wachtel, 6977926
Pvt William H. Wallace, 6978308
Pvt Benjamin Wentzel, 6977666
Pvt Barlow M. Wescott, 6977966
Pvt Robert F. Wheaton, 6977665

Pvt Rolland D. Perry, 6980365
Pvt James Pettyjohn, 6948729
Pvt Benny C. Picone, 6979196
Pvt Fred M. Pilger, 6974989
Pvt Richard E. Piper, 6982247
Pvt Bernard J. Polin, 6717165
Pvt Joseph D. Ponzillo, 6977979
Pvt William M. Wick, 6982065
Pvt Victor H. Woermer, 6978307
Pvt William R. Yaraschuck, 6903385
Pvt Edward C. Yess, Jr., 6979059
Pvt John H. Young, 6981457
Pvt Walter W. Zapko, 6981456
Pvt Joseph M. Zerbo, 6981310

Travel directed is necessary in the military service. Quartermaster Corps will furnish the necessary rail transportation, chargeable to FD 2437 P 1-0620 P 177-0620 P 50-0623 P 80-0600 P 82-0600 A 0410-0; QM 1620 P 72-0110, P 72-0284 P 72-1378 P 54-0700 P 61-0700 P 59-0700 A 0525-0 "D"; FD 1437 P 190-0623 A 0410-0. Travel by privately owned conveyance is authorized for such enlisted men as are not required to accompany the troops and detached service for not to exceed four days is authorized for travel time. Upon completion of this temporary duty, Lieutenant Colonel Douglas Johnston, Air Corps, First Lieutenant Lucio E. Gatto, Medical Corps Reserve, and Private 1cl Marvin Clark, R-1015172, Base Headquarters and 2nd Air Base Squadron (Single) GHQ Air Force, will return to their proper station, Mitchel Field, N.Y., for duty.

By order of Colonel NETHERWOOD:

OFFICIAL /s/ F. L. Vidal
F.L. VIDAL
1st Lieut, Air Corps,
Adjutant.

/s/ F. L. Vidal
F.L. VIDAL
1st Lieut, Air Corps,
Adjutant.

ABMFSO#88 (4-15-40)
CERTIFIED A TRUE COPY: JOHN R. JONES, 2nd Lt. A.C.

AIR BASE HEADQUARTERS
Barksdale Field

SPECIAL ORDERS Shreveport, Louisiana,
NO. 95) April 27, 1940

1. Pursuant to instructions contained in Letter, Hq, 4th C.A., file 370.5 General, dated April 23, 1940, the following named enlisted men, Quartermaster Corps, S.E. Air Base, attached to Detachment Quartermaster Corps, Barksdale Field, Louisiana, are relieved from attachment and are transferred and will proceed from Barksdale Field, Louisiana, on or about May 2, 1940, to MacDill Field, Tampa, Florida, by rail, for permanent station. Upon arrival at MacDill Field the following named enlisted men will report to the Commanding Officer for duty:

Pvt Manson Blackwell, 7008848
Pvt Elbert L. Brumfield, 7009178
Pvt Hirschel C. Carithers, 7009195
Pvt Jess V. Cook, 7002933
Pvt Winford M. Floyd, 7002891
Pvt Alvin E. Gore, 7008845
Pvt James B. Jolley, 7008851
Pvt Willie P. McGee, 7000820
Pvt Loyd T. Moore, 7002945
Pvt Louis C. Nall, 7002944
Pvt Roy E. Tucker, 7002916
Pvt Joe N. Simmons, 7009200
Pvt Sidford Walters, 7002932
Pvt Robert L. Whittekin, 7008852
Pvt Carmil L Box, 7008832
Pvt Theodore A. Brooks, 700967
Pvt Earl E. Coffman, 7008847
Pvt Lavelle Davis, 6390902
Pvt Hiram T. Gatewood, 7002873
Pvt James T. Holland, 7002938
Pvt Carlton l. Martinez, 7000679
Pvt John B. McNiece, 6391072
Pvt Felix J. Nall, 6307385
Pvt Hugh G. Patton, 7000821
Pvt Thomas B. Sadler, 7000879
Pvt Chester H. Stanley, 7000879
Pvt Walter S. West, 6378116
Pvt William L. Williams, 7008838

The Quartermaster Corps will furnish the necessary rail transportation.

Individual clothing and equipment will be taken by each enlisted man.

It being impracticable for the Government to furnish cooking facilities for rations, the Finance Department will pay, in advance, the monetary travel allowance prescribed in Table II, Par. 2a, C-4, AR 35-4520, at the rate of two dollars and twenty-five cents per day for rations for twenty-eight men for one and two-thirds (1 2/3) days.

The travel directed is necessary in the military service and payment when made is chargeable to procurement authorities: FD 1437 P 50-0623 A 0510-0; QM 1620 P 61-0700 P 72-0110 P 72-0284 P 72-1378 A 0525-0.

The Quartermaster and Finance Officers to whom expense accounts in connection with this order are submitted for payment will submit a detailed report by purpose numbers under each procurement authority to the Commanding Officer Barksdale Field, Louisiana, as soon as practicable after the above movement has been completed in accordance with par. 13, AR 35-1040.

2. Pursuant to instructions contained in Letter, WD, AGO, file AG 370.5 (4-19-40) E., dated April 19, 1940, the following named enlisted men, Detachment Medical Department, S.E. Air Base, attached to Detachment Medical Department, Barksdale Field, Louisiana, are relieved from attachment and are transferred in grade and with specialist ratings and will proceed from Barksdale Field, Louisiana, on or about May 2, 1940, to MacDill Field, Tampa, Florida, by rail for permanent station. Upon arrival at MacDill field the following named enlisted men will report to the Commanding Officer for duty:

Sgt Clifford W. Wisuer, 6384387 (In charge)
Pvt lcl Sp6cl Frank Masling, 7002896
Pvt Sp6cl Edison E. Cabaniss, 6970824
Pvt lcl Sp5cl Lee O. Cradic, 6813920
Pvt lcl Sp4cl Ray V. Wallace, 6792423
Pvt Frank T. Pikutis, 6815125

St Sgt Elmer Davis, 6065659 - now on furlough, address PO Box 1416, Ft Benning, Ga, authorized travel by privately owned conveyance, with detached service for two days for travel; to report to CO, MacDill Field, Florida, upon completion of furlough.

The Quartermaster Corps will furnish the necessary rail transportation.

Individual clothing and equipment will be taken by each enlisted man.

It being impracticable for the Government to furnish cooking facilities for rations, the Finance Department will pay, in advance, the monetary travel allowance prescribed in Table II, Par. 2a, C-4, AR 35-4520, at the rate of two dollars and twenty-five cents ($2.25) per day for rations for seven (7) men for one and two-thirds (1 2/3) days.

The travel directed in necessary in the military service and payment when made is chargeable to procurement authorities: FD 1437 P 50-0623 P 82-0600 A 0410-0; QM 1620 P 61-0700 P 72-0110 P 72-0284 P 72-1378 A 0525-0.

The Quartermaster and Finance Officers to whom expense accounts in connection with this order are submitted for payment will submit a detailed report by purpose numbers under each procurement authority to the Commanding Officer, Barksdale Field, Louisiana, as soon as practicable after the above movement has been completed, in accordance with Par. 13, AR 35-1040.

3. Pursuant to instructions contained in Letter, WD, AGO, file AG 370.5 (4-19-40) E., dated April 19, 1940, the following named enlisted men, Detachment Medical Department, S.E. Air

Base, attached to Detachment Medical Department, Barksdale Field, Louisiana, and now on detached service at Camp Beauregard, Louisiana, in connections with Third Army Maneuvers being conducted in that vicinity, are relieved from attachment and are transferred in grade and with specialist rating and will proceed from Barksdale Field, Louisiana, upon conclusion of maneuvers, to MacDill field, Tampa, Florida, by rail for permanent station. Upon arrival at MacDill Field the following named enlisted men will report to the Commanding Officer for duty:

Sgt Arthur C. Blue, Jr., 6925185
Pvt lcl Sp6cl Charles R. Myers, 6925193
Pvt lcl Sp6cl Richard F. Tinder 6658140
Pvt Thomas V. Atkins, 7002978
Pvt John Cappa, Jr., 7002993
Pvt Russell J. Gardiner, Jr., 7008811
Pvt Jessie D. New, 7008843
Pvt Earl W. Sewell, 7008826
Pvt Clarence O. Tyler, 7008810
Corp Robert O. Mobley, 6777635
Pvt lcl Sp4cl Charles E. Simpson, 6921367
Pvt Johnnie Atkins, 7008829
Pvt Lenvol G. Bowers, 7002994
Pvt Leo P. Charpentier, 7009155
Pvt Frank S. Holeton, 7002896
Pvt Quitman Rayborn, 7009107
Pvt Johnny Sharp, 7002929

The Quartermaster Corps will furnish the necessary rail transportation.

Individual clothing and equipment will be taken by each enlisted man.

It being impracticable for the Government to furnish cooking facilities for rations, the Finance Department will pay, in advance, the monetary travel allowance prescribed in Table II, Par. 2a, C-4, AR 35-4520, at the rate of two dollars and twenty-five cents ($2.25) per day for rations for seventeen (17) men for one and two-thirds (1 2/3) days.

The travel directed is necessary in the military service and payment when made is chargeable to procurement authorities: FD 1437 P 50-0623 P 82-0600 A 0410-0; QM 1620 P 61-0700 P 72-0110 P 72-0284 P 72-1378 A 0525-0.

The Quartermaster and Finance Officers to whom expense accounts in connection with this order are submitted for payment will submit a detailed report by purpose numbers under each procurement authority to the Commanding Officer, Barksdale Field, Louisiana, as soon as practicable after the above movement has been completed, in accordance with P:ar. 13, AR 35-1040.

By order of Colonel BRERETON:
/s/ E.W. Hampton
2nd Lt., Air Corps, Adjutant.

DISTRUBUTION:

"G" Plus:
150-Det QMC
50-Transportation Clerk, QMC
150-Det Med Dept
10-S/Sgt Elmer Davis (PO Box #1416, Ft Benning, Ga)
100-CO, MacDill Field, FL
5-2nd Lt Nolan
2-Extra copies FO (Par 5)
2-Extra copies Base QM (Par 5)
12-Pfc Watkins
S-CO, AC Training Det, Ala Institute of Aeronautics, Tuscaloosa, AL
25-Mr Sgt Faust
2-CO, March Field, CA

CERTIFIED A TRUE COPY:
JOHN R. JONES,
2nd Lt., Air Corps.

AIR BASE HEADQUARTERS
LANGLEY FIELD, VIRGINIA

(H-4/we)

May 14, 1940.

CORRECTED COPY:

SPECIAL ORDERS)

NUMBER 114…)

EXTRACT

3. Pursuant to authority contained in letter AG 370.5 (4-16-40) E from the adjutant General to the Commanding General, Third Corps Area, Baltimore, Maryland, subject "Orders", April 19, 1940, and instructions contained in 1st Ind. 220.33 QMC (4-19-40)22, Headquarters, 3rd Corps Area, April 24, 1940, the following named enlisted men of the Detachment Quartermaster Corps, this station, are transferred in grade and with specialist rating to MacDill Field, Florida, effective May 16, 1940, and will proceed on that date by rail from Langley Field, Virginia, to MacDill Field, Florida, reporting upon arrival thereat to the commanding officer for duty.

Sgt GEORGE E. HERPIN, 6021263 Sgt JAMES F. WHITE, R-3828071

Cpl WILLIAM W. SMITH, R-817815 Pvt JACK BERRY, 6890363

Pvt Sp 5cl ROBERT B. BYER, 6886657 Pvt JOSEPH J. COOK, 6995952

Pvt JOSEPH S. DeSALVO, 6947126 Pvt Michael S. DEWOSKI, 6770396

Pvt JOHN P. ESKRIDGE, 6998445 Pvt EDWARD E. GANTE, 6998332

Pvt FREDERICK HERTING, 6997827 Pvt MELVIN L. OSBOURNE, 6884173

Pvt Sp 2cl LYLE POLLEY, 6885172 Pvt LOUIS P. SONDAY, 6997757

Pvt CHARLES R. THORN, 6999714

It being impracticable for the Government to furnish cooking facilities for rations, the Finance Department will pay, in advance the monetary travel allowance prescribed in Table II, Par. 2a, C-4, AR 35-4520, at the rate of two dollars and twenty-five cents ($2.25) per day for rations for fifteen (15) men for one and one-thirds (1 1/3) days.

The travel directed is necessary in the military service and payment when made is chargeable to procurement authorities: FD 1437 P 50-0623 A 0410-0; QM 1620 P 61-0700 P 72-0110 P 72-0284 P 72-1378 A 0525-0.

By order of Colonel Wuest:

/s/ William G. Lee, Jr
WILLIAM G. LEE, JR.,
1st Lieut., Air Corps,
Adjutant

OFFICIAL:

CERTIFIED A TRUE COPY:

JOHN R. JONES
2nd Lt., Air Corps.

Distribution:
5 – CO, MacDill Field
25 – CO, Det QMC
1 – Personnel
1 – File

HEADQUARTERS AIR BASE
MacDill Field
Office of the Commanding Officer

Tampa, Florida
June 5, 1940

MINUTES OF A MEETING CALLED TO ORGANIZE A POST EXCHANGE

AT MacDILL FIELD, TAMPA, FLORIDA

1. The following eligibles, representing all organizations at MacDill Field, met at MacDill Field at 8:30 A.M., June 5, 1940.

Lt. Col. M. C. Grow, President	Det. Medical Corps
Maj. Louis Cansler, Member	Det., 5th Sig. Ser. Co., 9th Sig. Plat.
Maj. J. F. Greene, Member	238th Sep. Q.M. Co., Co. L, 30th Q.M. Bn. Co. D., 89th Q.M. Bn.
Maj. C. T. Skow, Post Exchange Officer	
Maj. C. E. O'Conner	Base Hqs. & 27th Air Base Sq.
Maj. H. P. Rush	6th Bomb Sq.
Maj. W. G. Bryte	Hqs. & Hqs. Sq., 29th Bomb Gp.
Capt. J. A. Samford	43rd Bomb Sq.
Capt. G. R. Barnes	3rd Plat., 333rd Ord. Co.

2. The President, Lt. Colonel Grow, turned the meeting over tot eh Post Exchange Officer.

3. The Post Exchange Officer announced that the purpose of the meeting was to organize a Post Exchange at MacDill Field.

4. It was moved, seconded and carried that the Exchange be organized based on a five dollar per share valuation.

5. The following statement of policy concerning initial expenditures for furniture and fixtures was adopted:

> That initially the general policy of expenditures for fixtures be on a conservative and economical basis because the tactic al squadrons do not wish to invest their funds excessively in frozen assets while world conditions are unsettled and there is little assurance that these squadrons will be based permanently at MacDill Field.

6. It was moved, seconded and carried that the Post Exchange operate without concessions.

7. After discussion, motion was made, seconded and carried that the Post Exchange activities include only the following:

> A general merchandise section including tobacco products, and bus, streetcar and theatre tickets.
>
> A beer bottled soft drinks section.
>
> A tailor shop including cleaning, pressing, and repairing.
>
> A shoe repair shop.
>
> A gas station to consist initially of two 10,000 - 12,000 gallon tanks and necessary related facilities. this equipment to be purchased by the Post Exchange and put in operation as soon as practicable.

The following activities were excluded: laundry, barber shop, restaurant, grocery and soda fountain.

The meeting having adjourned at 11:00 A.M., June 5, 1940, reconvened at 8:30 A.M., June 6, 1940.

8. A committee consisting of Major O'Conner, Major Rush, and Major Old, was appointed by the President to investigate the advisability of erecting an open screened pavilion west of the present Post Exchange building for use as a beer garden.

9. A committee consisting of Major O'Conner, Major Rush, and Major old was appointed by the President to investigate the advisability of establishing either a 29th bombardment Group Canteen or a MacDill Field branch Exchange at Drew Field.

10. The Post Exchange Officer was authorized to hire the following personnel initially and to augment this personnel as required and in accordance with business expansion: one steward, one bookkeeper-stenographer, one janitor, and three clerks.

11. All eligibles whose signatures appear on the next page desire to become initial members of the MacDill Field Post Exchange, and are submitting application for membership.

The signatures of the eligibles, representing all organizations at MacDill Field, appear below:

MALCOLM C. GROW
Lt. Colonel, Medical Corps, President

LOUIS CANSLER
Major, Signal Corps, Member

JAMES F. GREENE
Major, Quartermaster Corps, Member

CHARLES T. SKOW
Major, Air Corps, Post Exchange Officer

C.E. O'CONNER
Major, Air Corps, Member

HUGO P. RUSH
Major, Air Corps, Member

WALTER G. BRYTTE
Major, Air Corps, Member

JOHN A. SAMFORD
Captain, Air Corps, Member

GEORGE R BARNES
Captain, Infantry (Ord.), Member

WILLIAM D. OLD
Major, Air Corps

CONSTRUCTION PROGRAM AT AIR CORPS STATIONS NO. 3 MACDILL FIELD, TAMPA, FLORIDA, AIRPORT PROJECT JACKSONVILLE, FLORIDA DISTRICT

July 2, 1941

1. Location and general description of project:

MacDill Field Air Base is located six miles southeast of Tampa, Florida and occupies the southerly portion of Interbay Peninsula between Hillsborough, Old Tampa and Tampa Bay. The site is reached by paved highways and railroad, and by water by two shallow draft channels. The project now authorized contemplates the construction of buildings, structures, and facilities to house and serve Air Base Headquarters, two groups with attached air service squadrons, air base troops and service troops. The authorized troop strength is 460 officers and 5,183 enlisted men of all branches. Air Corps troops comprise about 70 percent of the total authorized strength. Construction of both permanent and temporary types is involved. There were no airport facilities previously existing at the site. The Air Corps began flying operations from the runways at MacDill Field on February 7, 1941.

2. Pertinent data:

a) The latest directives for MacDill field issued by the Adjutant General's Office to the Quartermaster General were dated August 2, 1940, and October 124, 1940, and to the Chief of Engineers, February 27, 1941.

b) Date plot plan approved by Air Corps: January 12, 1940; revised March 7, 1940.

c) Land procurement: Land procurement has been completed for MacDill as now authorized.

d) Tabulated herewith is list of the more important contracts and data pertaining to them:

CONTRACTS

Awarded	Approved	Structure
4-27-40	6-6-40	Photographic Laboratory
2-6-40	3-19-40	Non-Commissioned Officers Qtrs.
4-25-40	6-18-40	Fire & Guard House with Com. Ctr.
5-20-40	7-5-40	Four Warehouses
7-31-40	10-3-40	Five Single Field Officers Qtrs.
7-20-40	9-11-40	Runways
7-25-40	9-28-40	Air Corps Gas Fueling System
8-7-40	10-4-40	Hangars
8-26-40	9-28-40	Water Tank (500,000 gallons)

9-7-40	11-23-40	Electric Dist. & Street Lighting
9-10-40	11-28-40	Night Lighting System
11-20-40	12-31-40	Radio Transmitter building
12-7-40	2-1-40	Plumbing & Heating 96 Buildings Group
12-23-40	2-13-40	Dredging 75,000 cubic yards
1-16-41	1-18-41	Theatre
1-23-41	1-23-41	Radio Beacon Range Building
1-16-41	2-10-41	Plumbing & Heating, Hospital Group
3-11-41	3-15-41	Apron Additions
6-23-41	3-15-41	Chapels - 2
6-25-41	3-15-41	Fencing, North Boundary
6-27-41	3-15-41	Cold Storage - Q.M. Commissary and Warehouse
6-28-41	3-15-41	Armament, Instrument Inspection and Adjustment Building
6-30-41	3-15-41	Plumbing and Heating - 19 Buildings

Construction begun:

a) Administrative and housing 2-9-40

b) Hospital or Medical corps Installation 11-12-40

c) Technical facilities 6-27-40

3. Status of construction:

a) The status of construction of the major groups at MacDill Field on June 30, 1941, was:

Administration and housing.. 87%

Medical Corps Installation.. 100%

Technical 100%

Permanent construction 62%

Complete airfield... 70%

b) The buildings and facilities listed below have been completed and turned over to the control of The Commanding Officer, MacDill Field:

Temporary Type Construction

Administration and Housing:

Barracks, 63 men	73
Mess buildings, 250 men	18

A. C. storehouses	13
Warehouses	8
Administration buildings	7
Parachute building	1
Inflamable storage	1
Dayrooms	12
Officers Mess	2
Officers Quarters	5
Recreation Building	1
Post Exchange	1

Medical Corps Installation:

Barracks, 63 men	2
Mess Buildings, 250 men	1
Covered walk	1
Infirmary	1
Dental Clinic	1
Dayroom	1
Storehouses	2
Heating Plant	1
Wards	6
Administration Building	1
Nurses Quarters and Mess	1
Nurses Quarters	2
Officers Quarters and Mess	1

Technical:

Operations buildings	4

Permanent Construction

Non-commissioned officers quarters	3
Paint, oil, and dope storehouse	1
Signal and ordnance warehouse	1
Q. M. Warehouses	2
Q. M. Warehouse and commissary	1
Fire and Guardhouse with communication center	1
Field officers quarters	5
Steel water tank	1
Radio transmitter building	1
Railroad spur	1
Concrete runways and aprons	3

Gas meter house	1
AC oil storage system	1
Additional concrete aprons	2
A.C. Gasoline Fueling system	1
Motor Pool and QM Gasoline Station	3

4. Cost of project:

a) Authorized cost $6,576,852.00

b) Present estimated cost 6,687,841.81

c) Estimated cost of work under way or completed under authorized project 5,110,454.00

5. Funds allotted to date $6,950,400.07*

* - This amount includes $2,266,448.22 expended from allotments to the Quartermaster Corps.

6. Status of Plans and Specifications:

Plans and specifications are on hand for all authorized construction, except the permanent sewage treatment plant. These plans are now being prepared by consulting engineers.

7. Operations during this half-month period:

a) Construction work by contract was continued during the period on the items listed below. Construction involved in the buildings and structures listed is of permanent type, except the theater:

3 Hangars

1 electrical distribution and street lighting system

Plumbing and heating installations in 96 temporary building group and in Hospital group

1 Theatre

1 Radio Beacon Range Building

b) The night lighting system was placed in operation on February 9, 1941. A temporary control tower will be utilized until the permanent control tower is available on completion of the base hangar.

c) Work was also carried on throughout the period under W.P.A. projects on MacDill Field in which labor is furnished by that organization and materials and equipment by the War

Department, on the following items:

Fills:	Extensive earth filling operations throughout the building area.
Drainage:	Grading and drainage of lands.
Roadways:	Excavation, grading, placing and finishing lime rock, pouring concrete roadways and curbs on various roads and streets.
Grassplots:	Excavating, grubbing grading, and planting grassplots on airfield.
Water:	Connecting buildings to the water mains.
Sewer:	Building forms and pouring catch basins, etc., excavating and laying pipe for sanitary and storm sewers.
Temporary Construction:	Finishing work in 96 buildings group, including barracks, mess halls, Administration buildings, warehouses, post exchange, etc., and constructing Post Office and Service Club. construction continued on Service Club and Concrete was begun on 19 temporary buildings for additional Engineer troops.
Mixing Plant:	Mixing and pouring miscellaneous driveways to buildings, electric conduits, manholes, piers for buildings, catch basins, etc.
Dredging:	Pumping sand ashore to fill in low ground for building sites.
Electrical Distribution:	Excavating, setting forms, and pouring casings for electric conduits, manholes, backfilling, cleaning up manholes, etc. Filling around buildings and road construction.
Gas System:	Connecting new barracks and other buildings to the gas mains.

d) The structure listed below were completed and turned over to the control of the Commanding Officer, MacDill Field, during the period:

Permanent Construction:

Motor Pool and Q. M. Gasoline Station 3

e) Specifications were prepared and invitations for bids were issued for construction by contract of the items of new work listed below:

Underground Magazines and Ordnance Storage Facilities 20

Plumbing and Heating .... 19 Bldgs.

Kerosene, Gasoline, & Fuel Oil Storage and Dispensing System 1

f) Bids were opened and recommendations for award of contract were made for:

Chapels 2

Armament & Instrument Building 1

Fencing, North Boundary, Linear Feet 22,700

Cold Storage Rooms, Q.M. Commissary and Warehouse 3

Runway and Apron Extensions..3

Underground Magazines and Ordnance Storage Facilities..........................20

Plumbing and Heating..19

Kerosene, Gasoline, and Fuel Oil Storage and Dispensing System................1

g) Contracts were awarded for construction of:

Chapels..2

Fencing, North Boundary, Linear Feet (materials only).......................22,700

Cold Storage Rooms, Q.M. Commissary and Warehouse...........................3

Armament, Instrument Inspection and Adjustment Building.......................1

Plumbing and Heating..19

Magazines and Ordnance Storage Facilities..20

Kerosene, Gasoline, and Fuel Oil Storage..1

8. Probable operations next half month:

a) Construction by contract will continue on all items listed in paragraph 7a foregoing.

b) Construction and other operations will continue throughout the period on all W.P.A. works listed in paragraph 7c foregoing.

c) Contracts will be awarded for Runways and Apron Extensions.

9. Estimated date of completion:

a)	Administration and housing	8-31-41
b)	Medical Corps installation	Completed
c)	Technical facilities	Completed
d)	Permanent construction	2-28-42
e)	Project as a whole	2-28-42

Note: This project is occupied by troops. Facilities are in use and planes are operating from the runways. The dates shown above are for the complete field in accordance with the approved directive and authorized additional construction.

10. Remarks:

a) The work as a whole, including contract jobs and hired labor work under W.P.A.

projects is, with a few minor exceptions, up to schedule. No delays are expected, and it is contemplated that all work will be completed on or before the dates stated in paragraph 9 foregoing.

b) The total number of employees employed at this Air corps Project as of June 30, 1941, were as follows:

ITEM A	Architect Engineer	0
ITEM B	Constructing Contractor	122
ITEM C	W.P.A.	1,195
ITEM D	Project and District Engineers, H.L.	69
ITEM E	Project and District Engineers, Overhead	9
	Total employees	1,395

STATUS OF CONSTRUCTION PENDING AT AIR CORPS PROJECTS
JACKSONVILLE, FLA., DISTRICT

July 3, 1941.
3. MacDill Field, Fla.

Sewage Disposal Plant: Plans for sewage disposal plant at MacDill Field are being prepared by private consulting engineers, under contract for the design.

NOTE: This post has been occupied by the Air Corps. The time required for construction of the underground magazines will not materially affect operations by the Air Corps.

WAR DEPARTMENT. CORPS OF ENGINEERS, U. S. ARMY.

MAC DILL FIELD, TAMPA, FLORIDA
JACKSONVILLE, FLA. DISTRICT
CONSTRUCTION PROGRAM
PROGRESS CHART FOR PERIOD JUNE 16-30, 1941

LEGEND:

WORK COMPLETED PREVIOUSLY — — COMPLETED THIS HALF MONTH — — — PROBABLE NEXT HALF MONTH — —

IN 3 SHEETS SHEET NO. 1

ITEMS	NUMBER OR QUANTITY	PERCENT COMPLETED 10 20 30 40 50 60 70 80 90
ADM. AND HOUSING, GARRISON		
POST OFFICE (TEMP.)	1	
BARRACKS, STD.	73	
DAY ROOM, A-5 TYPE	1	
DAY ROOM, AC TYPE	11	
MESS, E.M., STD.	1	
MESS, E.M., AC TYPE	20	
MESS, OFFICERS, AC TYPE	2	
QUARTERS, OFFICERS	5	
ADMINISTRATION BLDG., A-8 TYPE	3	
ADMINISTRATION BLDG., A-12 TYPE	4	
SUPPLY ROOM, SA-2 TYPE	10	
POST EXCHANGE, E-3 TYPE	1	
WAREHOUSE, SH-18 TYPE	8	
STOREHOUSE	3	
OFFICE BLDG., A-21 TYPE	4	
OFFICE BLDG., A-16 TYPE	1	
PARACHUTE BUILDING	1	
INFLAMMABLE STORAGE	1	
CHAPEL (TEMP.)	2	
TEL. & TEL. INSTALLATION		
RECREATION BLDG.	1	
THEATER	1	
MOTOR REPAIR SHOP	1	
RAILROAD SPUR		
SEWAGE DISPOSAL		
GAS		
WATER		
SERVICE CLUB		
BARRACKS, STD.	7	
DAY ROOM, AC TYPE	2	
MESS, AC TYPE	2	
ADMINISTRATION BLDG., A-8 TYPE	2	
STOREHOUSE, SA-2 TYPE	2	

WAR DEPARTMENT. CORPS OF ENGINEERS, U. S. ARMY.

MAC DILL FIELD, TAMPA, FLORIDA
JACKSONVILLE, FLA. DISTRICT
CONSTRUCTION PROGRAM
PROGRESS CHART FOR PERIOD JUNE 16-30, 1941

LEGEND:
WORK COMPLETED PREVIOUSLY — COMPLETED THIS HALF MONTH — PROBABLE NEXT HALF MONTH

IN 3 SHEETS — SHEET NO. 2

ITEMS	NUMBER OR QUANTITY	PERCENT COMPLETED 10 20 30 40 50 60 70 80 90
MEDICAL CORPS INSTALLATION		
ADM. HOSPITAL, A-1 TYPE	1	
WARDS, STD.	6	
QUARTERS & MESS, OFFICERS	1	
QUARTERS & MESS, NURSES	1	
QUARTERS, NURSES	2	
STOREHOUSE	2	
DENTAL CLINIC	1	
MESS, HOSPITAL	1	
HEATING PLANT	1	
BARRACKS, STD.	2	
INFIRMARY	1	
DAY ROOM	1	
TECHNICAL		
OPERATIONS BLDG.	4	
PERMANENT CONSTRUCTION		
FIRE & GUARD HOUSE & COM. CENTER	1	
QUARTERS, N.C.O.	3	
PHOTOGRAPHIC LAB.	1	
Q.M. WAREHOUSE	3	
SIGNAL & ORD. WAREHOUSE	1	
MOTOR POOL	1	
Q.M. GAS STATION	1	
PAINT, OIL & DOPE STORAGE	1	
HANGARS	3	
WATER TANK, 500,000 GALS.	1	
QUARTERS, SINGLE FIELD OFFICERS	5	
APRONS		
RUNWAYS		
NIGHT LIGHTING SYSTEM		
ELEC. DIST. SYSTEM		
RADIO TRANSMITTER BLDG.	1	
A.C. OIL STORAGE SYSTEM		

WAR DEPARTMENT. CORPS OF ENGINEERS, U.S. ARMY.

MAC DILL FIELD, TAMPA, FLORIDA
JACKSONVILLE, FLA. DISTRICT
CONSTRUCTION PROGRAM
PROGRESS CHART FOR PERIOD JUNE 16-30, 1941

LEGEND:
WORK COMPLETED PREVIOUSLY — COMPLETED THIS HALF MONTH — PROBABLE NEXT HALF MONTH

IN 3 SHEETS SHEET NO. 3

ITEMS	NUMBER OR QUANTITY	PERCENT COMPLETED (10 20 30 40 50 60 70 80 90)
PERMANENT CONSTRUCTION		
A.C. FUELING SYSTEM		
APRON ADDITIONS		
RADIO BEACON RANGE BLDG.	1	
INSTRUMENT BUILDING	1	
RUNWAY EXT.		
APRON EXT.		
FLIGHT HANGARS	2	
DRAINAGE		
FENCING		
COLD STORAGE Q.M. COMM.		
GAS, KERO., FUEL OIL STORAGE		
MAG. & ORD. STORAGE		
A.C. FUELING SYSTEM - 2ND UNIT		
ADM. AND HOUSING, GARRISON		
MEDICAL CORPS INSTALLATION		
TECHNICAL		
PERMANENT CONSTRUCTION		
COMPLETE AIRFIELD		

July 16-31, 1941

CONSTRUCTION PROGRAM AT AIR CORPS STATIONS

DREW FIELD, TAMPA, FLA.

1. LOCATION AND GENERAL DESCRIPTION OF PROJECT:

   Drew Field is located 4.5 miles northwest of Tampa, Florida, and 7.5 miles north of MacDill Field. The project consists of the construction of an Air Corps Station at the site of a former municipal airport which had an allover grass landing area but no runways. the Field is to serve as a District and Wing Headquarters of the Air Corps, with an authorized Troop strength of 118 officers and 686 enlisted men of all branches.

2. PERTINENT DATA:

   Inclusive dates of directives issued by A.G.O. 10-21-40
   1-6-41
   5-19-41
   Date layout plan approved by Air Corps 11-14-40
   Revised 12-31-40
   Revised 1-2-41
   Lease of land approved .... Government owned *
   Troop capacity of housing:
   Completed 876
   Under Construction 0
   To be constructed 0
   To be constructed 0
   Number of troops occupying Station 429
   Construction begun:
   a) Administration and Housing 12-17-40
   b) Hospital or Medical Corps installation 12-17-40
   c) Technical Facilities 12-17-40

* See note under Paragraph 9, REMARKS

3. STATUS OF CONSTRUCTION:

   All of the original program except the Technical Facilities has been completed. Work is under way on all items of the Technical Facilities.

   The Additional Program consists of an officers mess on which construction will begin during the next period.

   Concerning land procurement, attention is invited to Paragraph 9 of this report, REMARKS.

Percentage of Completion:

	Original Program	Additional Program	Total Program
Administration and housing including utilities	100%	0%	97.7%
Hospital or Medical Corps Installation	100%	None	100%
Technical Facilities	25.4%	None	25.4%
Project as a whole	49.4%	0%	49.1%
Readiness for occupancy and use	49.4%	0%	49.1%

4. <u>AUTHORIZED AND ESTIMATED COST</u>:

	Original Program	Additional Program	Total Program
A. Authorized Cost	$509,250	17,040	526,290
B. Estimated Cost			
(1) Work constructed or in place	605,903	0	605,903
(2) Work underway	135,045	0	135,045
(3) Work authorized but not yet underway	763,350	10,981	774,331
Total estimated cost	$1,504,298	10,981	1,515,279

5. <u>STATUS OF PLANS AND SPECIFICATIONS</u>:
All plans and specifications have been completed.

6. <u>OPERATIONS DURING THIS HALF-MONTH PERIOD</u>:
Construction on the Administration and housing group of the original program was completed.

In the technical group the AC Shop(hangar) was completed. Work was continued on the Radio Control Tower, and on Grading and Draining of Aprons and Runways.

W.P.A. forces continued work on roads, field drainage, sanitary and storm sewers, sewage disposal plant, connecting completed buildings to gas mains clearing and grading of runways, and on a large drainage project adjacent to Drew Field into which the field drainage system will tie.

7. <u>PROBABLE OPERATIONS NEXT HALF-MONTH</u>:
Work will be continued on all uncompleted items of the original program. Work will be initiated on the Officers' Mess.

8. <u>ESTIMATED DATE OF COMPLETION</u>:

	Original Program	Additional Program
a) Administration and housing (including utilities)	7-31-41	9-15-41
b) Hospital or Medical Corps Installation	6-20-41	None
c) Technical facilities	12-15-41	None
d) Project as a whole	12-15-41	9-15-41
e) Readiness for Occupancy and Use	6-25-41	9-15-41

9. <u>REMARKS</u>:

Land Procurement: The situation concerning land procurement at Drew Field is covered in detail in a letter from this office to the Chief of Engineers, dated August 5, 1941, Subject: "Deeds to land, Drew Field."

July 16-31, 1941

DREW FIELD, TAMPA, FLORIDA

HOSPITAL DATA SHEET

1. Following is the status of construction of the Hospital Installation. Construction commenced, December 17, 1940:

Item	Type	No. Required	Work begun	Percent completed	Estimated completion date
Infirmary	Special	1	12-17-40	100	Completed

WAR DEPARTMENT — CORPS OF ENGINEERS, U. S. ARMY

DREW FIELD, TAMPA, FLORIDA
CHART FOR PERIOD JULY 16-31, 1941
ORIGINAL PROGRAM

LEGEND
WORK COMPLETED PREVIOUSLY
COMPLETED THIS HALF MONTH
PROBABLE NEXT HALF MONTH

MAP ITEM	ITEMS	TYPE	NUMBER OR QUANTITY	PERCENT COMPLETED (0 – 25 – 50 – 75 – 100)
	ADM. & HOUSING (INCL. UTIL.)			
1	ADM. BUILDING	A-8	3	
2	BARRACKS (63 MEN)	STD.	12	
3	DAY ROOM	AC	4	
4	GUARD HOUSE	GH-1	1	
5	MESS, EM.-500 MEN, CAFETERIA.	STD.	1	
6	MESS, EM.-250 MEN	STD.	1	
7	MESS, OFFICERS	AC	1	
8	ADM. BUILDING	A-12	2	
9	POST EXCHANGE	E-2	1	
10	QUARTER, OFFICERS	OQ-40	3	
11	MOTOR REPAIR SHOP	SP-1	1	
12	FIRE STATION	F-2	1	
13	WAREHOUSE	SA-2	4	
14	WAREHOUSE	SH-9	1	
15	TELEPHONE & TELEGRAPH BLDG.	TT-2	1	
16	GASOLINE STORAGE, QM		1	
	TEL. & TEL. INSTALLATION		JOB	
	GAS SYSTEM		JOB	
	WATER SYSTEM		JOB	
	ELECTRICAL SYSTEM		JOB	
	SEWAGE DISPOSAL		JOB	
	SEWAGE TREATMENT PLANT		JOB	
	TOTAL ADM. & HOUSING			
	HOSPITAL OR MEDICAL CORPS INSTALLATION			
17	INFIRMARY	SP	1	
	TOTAL MEDICAL CORPS			
	TECHNICAL			
18	AC GAS & OIL STORAGE		1	
19	MAG. PYRO. STORAGE	SH-10	1	
20	OPERATIONS BLDG.	A-12	1	
21	RADIO CONTROL TOWER		1	
22	SHOP-AC HANGAR		1	
	APRON:			
	GRADING		JOB	
	DRAINAGE		JOB	
	PAVING		JOB	

SHEET NO. 1

WAR DEPARTMEN.

CORPS OF ENGINEERS. U. S. ARMY

DREW FIELD, TAMPA, FLORIDA.

CHART FOR PERIOD JULY 16-31, 1941

ADDITIONAL PROGRAM

LEGEND

WORK COMPLETED PREVIOUSLY

COMPLETED THIS HALF MONTH

PROBABLE NEXT HALF MONTH

MAP ITEM	ITEMS	TYPE	NUMBER OR QUANTITY	PERCENT COMPLETED 0 25 50 75 100
	ADM. & HOUSING			
23	MESS, OFFICERS	OM-1	1	
	TOTAL ADM. & HOUSING			
	PERCENT COMPLETED (ADDITIONAL PROGRAM)	OM-		
	PERCENT OF READINESS FOR OCCUPANCY AND USE (ADDITIONAL PROGRAM)			
	PROJECT AS A WHOLE (ORIGINAL PROGRAM PLUS ADDITIONAL PROGRAM)			

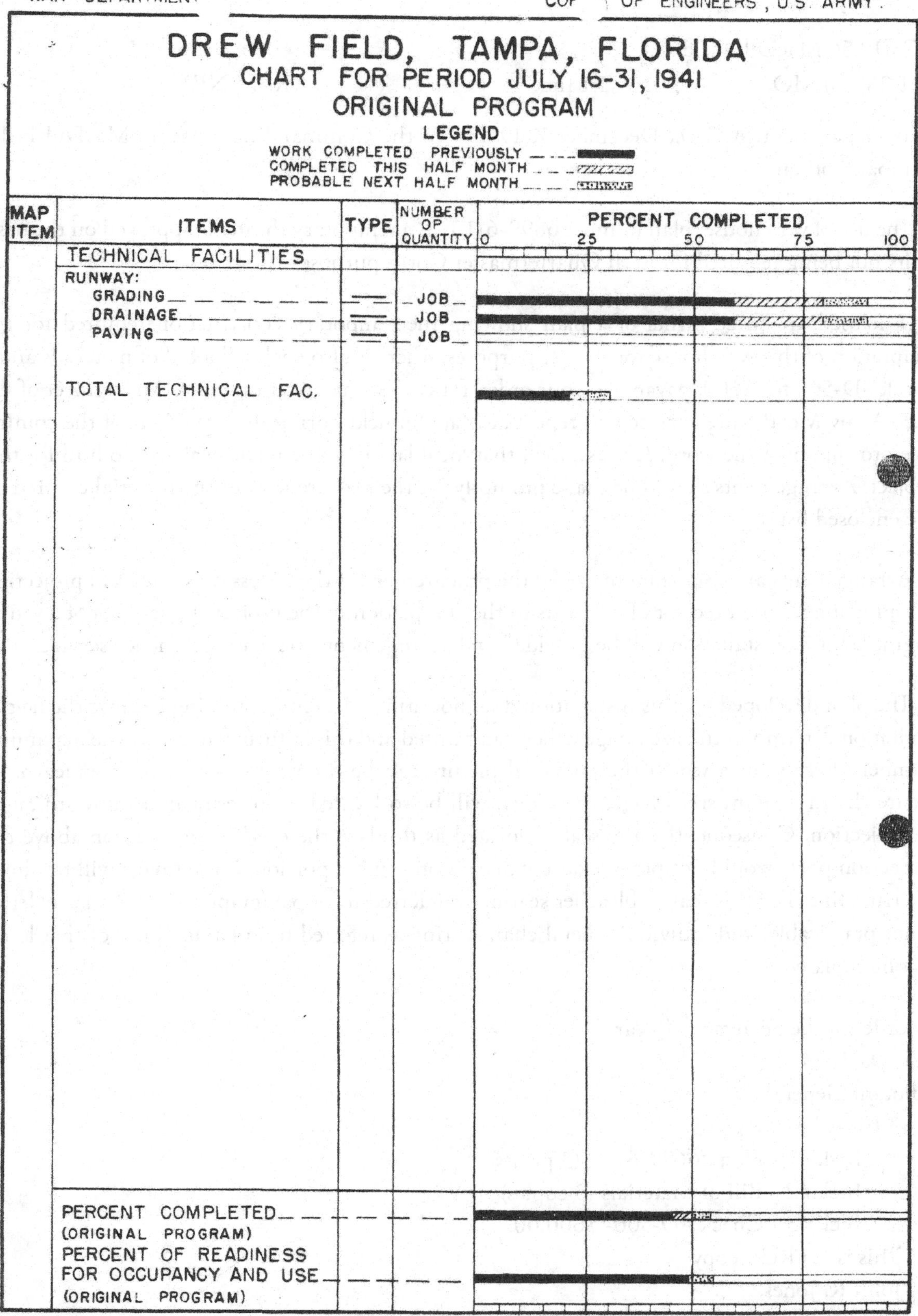

WAR DEPARTMENT — CHIEF OF ENGINEERS, U.S. ARMY

DREW FIELD, TAMPA, FLORIDA
CHART FOR PERIOD JULY 16-31, 1941
ORIGINAL PROGRAM

LEGEND
WORK COMPLETED PREVIOUSLY
COMPLETED THIS HALF MONTH
PROBABLE NEXT HALF MONTH

MAP ITEM	ITEMS	TYPE	NUMBER OF QUANTITY	PERCENT COMPLETED 0 25 50 75 100
	TECHNICAL FACILITIES			
	RUNWAY:			
	GRADING	—	JOB	
	DRAINAGE	—	JOB	
	PAVING	—	JOB	
	TOTAL TECHNICAL FAC.			
	PERCENT COMPLETED (ORIGINAL PROGRAM)			
	PERCENT OF READINESS FOR OCCUPANCY AND USE (ORIGINAL PROGRAM)			

SHEET NO. 2

CONFIRMATION COPY -- ORIGINAL SENT BY AIR MAIL

AG 413.56 MacDill Field
(11-28-40) MO 1st Ind. RBM:NEN

War Department, A.G.O., December 7, 1940 - To the Commanding General, MacDill Field, Tampa, Florida.

1. The use of warehouse, plan number 6899-611.1, as a temporary theater is approved on the basis of its not being required for local Quartermaster Corps purposes.

2. Enclosed are three prints of a plan showing the temporary construction required for the adaptation of this warehouse for theater purposes. There is also enclosed a bill of materials and a check #D-500 for $600, payable to your order, for the estimated cost thereof. An engineer of the U.S. Army Mo-Picture Service will report at MacDill field during the latter part of the coming week to supervise the work. It is assumed that local labor can be made available to him for this project. Arrangements should be made promptly for the procurement of the material covered by the enclosed list.

3. Arrangements are also being made for the procurement of the necessary sound and projection equipment and upon receipt of advise as to the completion of the project the services of a sound engineer for its installation will be provided and arrangements made to commence service.

4. The plan developed for this installation does not utilize the entire building because the height limitation determines the size image which can be used and this in turn determines the maximum number of seats from which the projected picture can be properly viewed. In an endeavor to secure the maximum size image, the screen will be so located as to result in an upward angle of projection. Consequently, any seat so located as to place the eye line of a person above the projection ports would not provide acceptable vision, since a portion of the image will be above the truss line. For this reason bleacher seating as referred to in paragraph 3-c of the basic letter is not practicable, and individual metal chair seating as referred to in paragraph 1 of that letter is contemplated.

By order of the Secretary of War:
T. J. Davis
Adjutant General

3 Incls.:

Incl. #1 - Plan #6699-611.1 (3 prints)
Incl. #2 - Bill of Materials (3 copies)
Incl. #3 - Check #D-500- $600.00.

This is a TRUE copy
John R. Jones
2nd Lt., Air Corps, Historical Officer

STATION HOSPITAL
MacDILL FIELD
FLORIDA

December 21, 1940

SUBJECT: Special Sanitary Report; Prophylactic Stations in the City of Tampa

TO: The Surgeon, Station Hospital, MacDill Field, Florida

1. The two prophylactic stations in the City of Tampa, one for white soldiers and one for negro soldiers, and the room in the Enlisted Men's Club, to which the station for white soldiers is to be moved, were inspected on December 19, 1940.
   a) Prophylactic Station for White Soldiers: this station is located in the building of the Health Department of the City of Tampa at the corner of Tampa and Scott Streets. the toilet in use for prophylaxis, in which there is a lavatory and a urinal, is satisfactory in every way. The toilet was quite clean. The equipment for prophylaxis was not in sight. Then enlisted personnel on duty at this station were not on duty at the time the inspection was made. Dr. J. R. McEachern, City Health Officer, mentioned that the conduct of the enlisted personnel on duty has been satisfactory in every way.
   b) Prophylactic Station for Negro Soldiers: This station is located at 1003 1/2 Scott Street, in a small room which adjoins and connects with a negro physician's officers. Dr. J. A. White, the negro physician, has given the use of this room without compensation. The room is satisfactory in every particular except one. It is difficult to find. The entrance to Dr. White's offices, which are upstairs, is by an outside stairway which is unmarked by either a sign or a number. The station was clean and the equipment and furnishings were in good order. The enlisted personnel assigned to this station were not on duty at the time the inspection was made.
   c) Station to be established at the Enlisted Men's Club: A urinal must be installed in the room provided for prophylaxis before the station now in operation in the building of the Tampa Health Department can be moved to the Enlisted Men's Club. Water and sewer connections can be made to those lines which are now connected to a lavatory in this room. Because the Enlisted Men's Club closes at midnight, this station cannot be used after that hour unless this regulation is changed.

2. Recommendations:
   a) Recommendation is made that Dr. J. A. White who has given a room at 1003 1/2 Scott Street for use as a prophylactic station for negro soldiers be paid a small sum each month to cover the cost of utilities - heat, lights and water. Suggestion is made that this sum be $5.00.
   b) Recommendation is made that the prophylactic station for negro soldiers be marked by a sign or a light.
   c) Recommendation is made that an outside entrance be provided for the prophylactic

station to be established at the Enlisted Men's Club. this can be done at small expense by converting a window, which opens on a side street, into a door. This will make it unnecessary to keep the club open after midnight. Application for permission to make this alteration may be made to the Mayor and to the Building Inspector of the City of Tampa.

/s/ J. J. Spencer
Major, M. C.
Base Medical Inspector
1st Ind. M/LKP/NTB
Station Hospital, Office of the Surgeon, MacDill field, Florida, December 24, 1940. TO: The commanding General, MacDill field, Florida.

Approved

For the Surgeon.

/s/ L. K. Pohl
Captain Medical Corps,
Executive Officer.

2nd Ind. H:ILS

AIRBASE HEADQUARTERS, MacDill Field, Florida, Dec 27, 1940. To:

The Surgeon, Station Hospital, MacDill Field, Florida.

1. Report noted.
2. Action on recommendation, paragraph 2c, being taken by Base Quartermaster through S-4 (Materiel) office.
3. Recommendations covered in paragraphs 2a and 2b will be present to organizations concerned, as regulations will not permit expenditure on building of this type by Quartermaster.

By command of Brigadier General TINKER:

H. H. YOUNG
Colonel, Air Corps
Executive

Copy withdrawn
4 S-4 Offices
This is a TRUE COPY
JOHN R. JONES
2nd Lt., Air Corps
Historical Officer

HISTORICAL SUMMARY OF MACDILL FIELD

(By Colonel H. H. Young, A-1, Third Air Force)

MacDill field was established under the Wilcox Act passed by Congress in 1935. The bill, known as the Wilcox Act, was sponsored by Congressman Wilcox of Florida. It provided for the establishment of several additional large air bases in the continental United States. to the best of my recollection, the site for MacDill Field was selected by a special War Department committee in 1936. However, actual construction was not started until late 1939. In the fall of 1939, Lt. Colonel Lynwood Jacobs of the Army Air Corps and Major Simpson of the Construction Quartermaster Department came to Tampa for the purpose of surveying the site and arranged for a layout plan of the installations, and certain clearing operations were initiated at that time. Actual construction was not started until about the first of the year, 1940. The first detachment of approximately fifty men arrived at MacDill field from Barksdale Field mid-March, 1940, at which time the undersigned arrived from Washington to assume temporary command of the field, pending arrival of General Tinker, Then Colonel Tinker. At this time, although construction was underway, no buildings had been actually completed and the detachment of fifty men above mentioned were being housed in the Public Health Service buildings in the present hospital area, while the city of Tampa provided office space in the City hall for a temporary headquarters for MacDill Field activities. On or about the first of April, a number of barracks were completed and the base detachment was moved from the buildings at Gadsden Point to the present barracks area and the headquarters was moved from the City Hall in Tampa to one of the barracks at MacDill Field. Temporary utilities such as water and electricity were available, but gas and sewerage were not installed until several weeks later. In the meantime, temporary provisions had to be made for cooking and for sewerage.

One of the major difficulties in the early operation at MacDill Field was the lack of usable roads, resulting in much wear and heavy maintenance requirements on all motor vehicle transportation.

Colonel Tinker arrived to assume command of MacDill field about May 24th 1940, and shortly thereafter the first tactical unit, the 29th bombardment Group, arrived from Langley Field, Virginia, for station at MacDill. Since the flying field was not yet in operation, the troops were housed at MacDill; flying operations for this group conducted from Drew Field. In the meantime construction was continued at MacDill field and included hangars, warehouses, barracks, administration buildings and runways.

To the best of my recollection, three runways were completed and MacDill Field therefore ready for air operations in February, 1941, at which time all flight operations pertaining to MacDill field were moved from Drew Field. concurrently with other construction, the hospital site was also built up using the existing Public Health Service buildings for the hospital administrative installations and adding to it the necessary number of word buildings. The boat basin in the hospital area at Gadsden Point, though still in use by the Public Health Quarantine Service, was also used as a base for ht rescue boats assigned to MacDill field.

Since the initial construction at MacDill Field took place under peacetime conditions when economy was the guiding rule, a limestone road system rather than concrete was installed. In connection with the road system for MacDill field, it was found that the approach roads to MacDill Field from Tampa were inadequate, because they were too narrow and had not been designed for the heavy traffic resulting from the operations of MacDill Field. To remedy this situation Hills Avenue, not MacDill Avenue, was closed for reconstruction and widening. When this road had been completed, the Bay shore Road was similarly reconditioned and a project for paving Vera Street, now Dale Mabry Highway, was initiated with a view to use of this highway as the main traffic road between MacDill field and Drew Field, and to connect with the state highway at Hillsboro Avenue. Another road was built across the north end of the MacDill Field reservation in order to gain access to the Port Tampa dock facilities.

MacDill Field was initially planned and established for a garrison of slight less than two thousand men, which would include one bombardment group. However, with the expansion of the Air Corps and other military services because of the war in Europe, MacDill Field continued to expand and by mid-summer, 1942, the garrison had mushroomed to more than 12,000 men. It might be interesting to list one of the key personnel during the early expansion state of MacDill Field. As indicated above, Colonel Jacobs was ordered to Tampa in the early fall of 1939, as a project officer for the construction of MacDill Field; Colonel Young assumed temporary command mid-march 1940; General Tinker, Then colonel Tinker, assumed command about 1 May 1940; General Bradley assumed command in July 1941; Colonel Young assumed command about 1 August 1941. In connection with construction project, the following is a resume of officers in charge. As indicated above, Major Simpson, Construction Quartermaster, reported to Tampa in the early fall, 1939. Major Robert Johnston relieved Major Simpson about 1 April 1940. When construction activities were assumed by the Chief of Engineers instead of the Construction Quartermaster, Major Reynolds Burt, now Colonel Burt, relieved Major Johnston and upon his departure for overseas was relieved by Captain Brown.

The initial Base Quartermaster was Major Dill, now Colonel Dill, who, upon activation of the 3rd Air Force Headquarters in Tampa, was designated as 3rd Air Force Quartermaster and relieved at MacDill Field by Colonel Witcher, then Major Witcher. The initial Base Surgeon was Colonel Malcolm Grow, now General Grow, who, upon being assigned 3rd Air Force Surgeon, was succeeded by Colonel Harrison Fisher. The initial Base Signal Officer was Captain Cansler, now Colonel Cansler, who, upon being assigned 3rd Air Force Signal Officer, was succeeded by Captain Phillips.

MacDill Field has the distinction of being the first Air Corps station used as a port of aerial embarkation for processing and dispatching airplanes to the combat zone in Europe. During the period 25 December 1941, to early February, 1942, approximately one hundred aircraft were processed at MacDill Field and departed from these to the European war zone by way of Trinidad, Natal, Brazil and Africa. The processing involved the preparation of personnel for overseas service, including personnel records, immunization, completion of personnel equipment, arrangements for entry in and passing through foreign ports and a complete check of the equipment to assure that airplanes upon leaving MacDill Field were in every way ready for combat. This involved, among other things, considerable work on gun turrets and machine guns in order to place this equipment in functional condition. It was also necessary to check weight and balance of each airplane prior to departure and finally the briefing of the crews for the flight from MacDill to Trinidad, South America. Each crew before leaving, in addition to being briefed for the flight, was furnished with a considerable amount of cash to defray expenses in route. Also included in this project was the shipment of $2,000,000 in cash for delivery to disbursement offices in the war zone. Shipment of this cash was made in four increments of one-half million dollars each. This shipment was accomplished insofar as flight between here and Trinidad was concerned without loss of life and with a loss of only one airplane.

A resume of the early activities of MacDill Field would not be complete without mention of the splendid assistance and cooperation extended by the city of Tampa, both by the city officials and the citizens of Tampa: First, in making the site of MacDill Field available for Army Air Corps use; by extending a whole-hearted welcome to all military personnel assigned to MacDill Field; by making available to MacDill Field personnel a building in town for use as an enlisted men's club (this was prior to the days of USO), and by continued active interest in the welfare of the military personnel stationed here.

Special mention might also be made of the splendid cooperation and service furnished by the Tamiami Trail Bus Company in furnishing public transportation between MacDill Field and Tampa at reasonable prices--this especially during the early construction period of MacDill Field, when, because of poor roads, maintenance of bus equipment was especially expensive.

One more item worthy of mention is the cooperation of the Tampa Electric Company in providing electric service at MacDill Field, meeting the ever changing and increasing demands of MacDill Field, and especially their cooperation in the removal of a high tension line on the north end of Drew Field, when this field was used as the flying field for MacDill. The removal of this line was accomplished by the electric company without hesitation, without delay and at their own expense.

/s/ H. H. Young

INTERVIEW WITH MR. O. P. CANNON

In order to translate the Southeastern Air Base from paper to the field two fundamental tasks had to be accomplished. The first of these was to survey and map the site and layout markers in accordance with the plans that had been approved by the Quartermaster Corps and the Office of the Chief of Air Corp in Washington. This task was carried out by the Constructing Quartermaster Corps of Engineers and was the immediate responsibility of Mr. Louis Ebling under the supervision of Major Lawrence L. Simpson, Q.M.C. The surveying crew was moved onto the site to commence this work in the latter half of September 1939. Six weeks later the second task was begun. This consisted of clearing the land and laying out the roads so that the actual construction work could begin. This was the work undertaken by the WPA under the supervision of Mr. O.P. Cannon.

It was on the morning of November 9, 1939 that Mr. Cannon and his crew of WPA workers arrived on the field. The site faced the men on that morning was hardly one that would permit them to see a field from which the great war planes could take off and land, where a large number of men could be housed and fed. They were faced with a typical Florida waste land consisting of palmettos, scrub pine, oak trees and swamps. It was to be in this jungle, with the occasional clearing for houses and a small field or two, that these men were to start the foundation work for a modern airbase.

The first job that they were called upon to perform was to clear the way for temporary roads that they would have to construct in order to get the necessary machinery and supplies to the areas of the field where construction was to begin. The first of these temporary roads was begun at what is now the MacDill Gate and ran down the line that had been named MacDill Avenue. At the point where the present MacDill Avenue, then Lisbon Avenue, stops, the road turned to the South, skirting the Southeastern end of the Northeast-Southwest runway and curving Eastward again. It ran to the present site of hangar number 5. There it took a Southerly direction to the site of the present Post Exchange where it terminated. This road was joined by the second road to be built that is now known as Florida Avenue, then Fourth Street. This road ran from the present site of the Post Exchange to the Bayshore Road, the latter being a road that was already in existence when the field was begun. Another road was built along the North boundary from the site of the present MacDill gate to the old Bayshore Road, and completing a circulatory system of roads that connected the two principal roads coming from Tampa with the purposed building area. The North boundary road was further developed as so to run Westward to the present laundry area.

This latter road provided access to the highest ground on the site directly from Lisbon Avenue Gate where the building officers were located with the area selected for a "borrow pit" to provide fill for the marshy spots in the barracks, hangar and runway areas. Still another road connected this "borrow pit" with the other road running over to the building area from the Hillsborough Road Gate. The completion of these temporary roads provided an interlocking system that gave access to every key point of the field that was to be utilized in the first construction program.

It was probably the temporary road-building program that first brought the builders of the Southeastern Air Base in grips with one of the most difficult problems that the builders had to face in constructing the project. This was the problem posed by the character of the soil on the site. Of course its characteristics were well understood before the work was ever begun, but it still remained the most persistent obstacle to be overcome. The character of the soil on the Base is very peculiar. It has been described as a "bodiless sand" which gives when dry the reaction usually found in round or "ball-bearing" grains of sand. But when it is wet "it's like dough". Whether it was wet or dry, the result was the same -- the vehicles were unable to get traction and men had great difficulty in getting around. In fact it goes further than that. The dry, shifting sand-like soil got into every crevice and crack and ruined machinery and surfaces of all kinds by leaving a gritty film everywhere. When the wind blew it made life almost unbearable. When the weather was wet and rainy, the mud was everywhere. Men brought it into the buildings on their feet and then it could hardly be cleaned out. And always it was holding up the transportation of machinery and building supplies. Obviously the malignant perversity of the soil cannot be considered an engineering problem only, it was a burden to be borne by all that worked for the completion of the field.

The discomfort that came to laborers and supervisors alike in constructing the Base because of the soil were not the only burdens to their existence. The site of the Southeastern Air Base was cursed with all of the pests familiar to such waste lands in Florida. Clouds of mosquitoes would molest the workmen at their duties and more exciting if not more annoying, were the myriads of snakes of all kinds. An almost unbelievable number of incredible huge and vicious diamond-back rattlers were killed during the course of construction. In fact snake killing was merely one of the additional duties everyone had to share. Many of these reptiles measured over six feet long and might be considered one of the occupational hazards connected with the construction of the field. In spite of the thousands of snakes that inhabited the field and the face that there were over 5000 civilians employed in the first construction program, there was not one case of snake bite recorded for the entire time that the project was underway. No doubt a real tribute to the average Floridian's skill in dealing with snakes.

When the roads were finished, the next step was to clear the sites that were to be used for runways and buildings. In completing this task as in the case of the roads as well, the cooperation of the construction Quartermaster Corps of Engineers and the WPA made it possible to expedite the work as rapidly as was compatible with thoroughness. Possibly the local as well as temporary nature of WPA had made it impractical for it to own the expensive and heavy equipment generally employed for the construction of large building projects such as the Southeaster Air Base. On the other hand, the Constructing Quartermaster Corps of Engineers was a permanent organization that had made a specialty of just such tasks. For that reason then, the Constructing Quartermaster Corps had plenty of such equipment ready to turn over to the WPA. The WPA in its turn had the manpower necessary for such projects and Quartermaster Corps did not. Furthermore, by employing funds allocated for WPA labor, the Army would be able to build more extensively because of its saving on labor costs. The two also cooperated in purchasing supplies, the quartermaster was able to supply the materials necessary for the buildings while the WPA supplied road materials such as brick for sewers, manholes and underground ducts for the utilities; cement, gravel and sand and oil for roads, sidewalks and building foundations. Again making it possible to spend even more money for the field than was actually allotted for the construction of the Base.

In clearing the field for construction it was necessary to have a system of ditches to drain the water especially from the site where the barracks were to be built. This site approached the actual swamp that lay between the high ground on the Northwestern side of the field and the old Bayshore Road that had been built out to the Quarantine Station at the tip of the peninsula. While there were some bad spots where the runways were to be located, the barracks area was especially bad. it would have been possible to have located the barracks area along the North boundary where there would have been sufficient high ground for the building necessary for the field even after expansion and shifting field even after expansion and shifting the runways toward the Southwest. This recommendation, which had been made by the engineers on the field, was rejected in favor of filling in the marshy ground and bringing the building area nearer the water front where it would be cooler as well as more beautiful. Furthermore, the swamp land would very likely have to be filled in at some time and it was possibly considered that it might as well be done as construction progressed. Whatever may have been the reasoning the dictated the final selection of the building area, the fact remained that it was swampy and draining was a necessity. Likewise, a great deal of fill would have to be brought in to make it usable, as the ground would have to be raised to four feet throughout the building area. Fortunately for the project a complete network of ditches had been dug during the Florida boom days be the Inter Bay Drainage District, one of many political subdivisions created by the State to carry on such projects. At that time a considerable part of the site had been laid out as building lots, separated by graded roads and even sidewalks complete with curbs. In order to turn this property into usable building sites, the drainage ditches had been dug and their cost charged against the property, costs that have not yet been paid in full. This system consisted of two large ditches into which many smaller ones fed their quota of swamp water. The main ditch for this building area started at a point close to the junction of the road from the "borrow pit". From this point, the ditch ran to the South, crossing the Northeast-Southwest runway, then the ditch turned in an Easterly direction and roughly parallelling the road to the building area. Near the start of the first permanent barracks area the ditch turned still further to the East so that it ran directly in front of the barracks area and in back of the present site of the Post Exchange and theatre buildings. Then making a right angled turn it ran to the end of the line of barracks where it turned again at right angles and ran in the Bay. The other ditch, known as the "old S--B--Ditch", started at a pond West of the "borrow pit" and ran toward the South. About 1500 feet from its beginning it was joined by another ditch that started at the extreme Western boundary. From this point the ditch continued directly to the South until its water entered the bay in the vicinity of the hospital area. These two ditches, with their subsidiary ditches, provided sufficient drainage for the area and was one more item that did not have to be paid for out of the funds appropriated for the base.

The first building program called for land to be cleared in three different areas. The first one to be cleared was the area used for the offices and sheds for the engineers and WPA officials as the Hillsborough gate, the second one were the runway areas, roughing out the Northeast-Southwest runway and the East-West runway. The third area to be cleared was the site for the permanent barracks area. The method of clearing these areas was to remove the trees and palmettos and then disc the ground thoroughly. The result was that the ground looked like a plowed field, but it was successful in eradication the roots and preparing the way for the building that was to follow.

In clearing the areas, the swampy ground had to be eliminated so as to provide a firm foundation for the buildings. In order to accomplish this task of eliminating swamp land it was necessary to dig out the much and refill with good sand form the "borrow pit". The drainage provided the sand base and the sewage system drained the rain water and eliminated the soft ground. Some idea of the size of these operations can be gained from the fact that over one hundred thousand tons of much was removed from the swampy ground where Hangar Number Three and its apron is now located.

A very important by-product to this work was the lumber that was produced from the trees that were removed. One of the first installations made on the field was a small saw-mill that was used to cut up the logs that were brought in from the clearings. These logs were turned into rough lumber that was used to erect the temporary buildings and sheeting for the underground ducts and sewers. Over a million board feet of lumber was cut in the sawmill, saving large sums of money for the rough lumber that would have to be used for construction purposes.

On the 15th of January 1940 the first directive arrived authorizing the construction of the first permanent buildings on the field. Under this directive thirty-one buildings were to be put up to house the first troops that were to be assigned to the field, and were to be completed around the Fifteenth of April. Included in this group of buildings were to be seventeen barracks to house sixty three men each, eight mess halls to handle one hundred men each and six day rooms. Work was commenced immediately on receipt of authorization and the actual building of the field was underway. Simultaneously work was begun on the railroad spur that was to run from the main line of Port Tampa. This spur was to be brought to the area now known as the "Vital Area". There it would be close to the barracks area and be able to supply the great hangars that were to be built later on.

February saw the first contracts being let to private contractors for the construction of other permanent installations on the field. A. J. Honeycutt Company received the first one that was let to build the three non-commissioned officers' quarters. Then followed contracts for the building of warehouses of Utilities, and Quartermaster Storage, the Fire house and Photographic Laboratory. Then contracts were let to the Central Construction Company to build the Base Hangar the two flight hangars, now hangars number Two and Three. The work was pushed along rapidly and the barracks were ready for occupancy when the first troops arrived on the 24th of April with the exception of the sewerage system which was completed about one month later.

During this early period of construction there was some difficulty experienced in getting some of the residents to leave their homes and plots of ground. One instance was the reluctance of a family to leave their home which was situated astride the line laid out for the railroad spur. This forced the engineers to make a curve around the house. When the road was completed and trains began to move over the tracks, the residents decided to move out of their home. Other than that, there was little difficulty experienced in getting people to move so that construction was the Benjamin House situated close to the Bayshore Road near Catfish Point. This house, built of cement stucco, was retained to be utilized as the first Officers' club and later as an Officers' Quarters. Aside from these there were about four houses that were occupied when the Army took title to the Base.

In March of 1940 work was started on a small dredge to dredge out sand from the Bay and provide a channel for the boats to be stationed at the dock for use as crash boats and receiving of supplies. After much bad luck that included burning of one dredge and a bad storm that blew another out into the bay, the dredge was completed and began to work in August of 1940. In operation, the dredge proved to be too small for the amount of work that had to be done, so after pumping about a thousand yards of sand from the bay into the parade ground area, it was taken off the job and sent around to hospital area where it was used to fill in the section where the nurses quarters were later built. Then in

December of 1941, the dredge known as the Dade was brought on the job to complete the work so begun. This dredge, owned by a West Palm Beach Firm, quickly finished the work and by January of 1941 the fill for Eastern or Headquarters Area had sufficient fill to bring the ground up to the level that was necessary for construction. In addition to that dredge deposited a great sand pile that was used to fill in around the barracks and in other places where fill material was required.

About July of 1940 the first housing problem arose for the Base. At this time the Air corps sent in about 2500 to 3000 men to be assigned to the Base. The building program had not yet provided for an increase of that size so the famous "Boom town" was created. "Boom Town" was a tent city that was constructed in the area of Chapel number Two and hangar Number Two, and was destined to be a feature of the camp that was to last for well over a year and a part of the Base that was to be the most vividly remembered by the men who had to live there. That first summer was an unusually wet one and the filling operations were far from complete. As a result the area was largely under water a good bit of the time and the men were never able to get their feet dry. Mud and water seemed to be the order of the day for that first summer. Then in the fall the situation was reversed with the onset of dry weather. At that time the sand blew with every puff of wind and tent life was plagued with sand in everything. At night the men wouldn't be able to sleep because of the sand in their blankets and during the day they couldn't eat because of the sand in their mess kits, nor walk because of sand in their shoes. That was the "Boom Town" whose passing brought great rejoicing on the Base.

HISTORICAL DATA SUPPLIED BY COLONEL LLOYD BARNETT

I got my first view of what was to be MacDill Field in the month of December, 1939 -- at which time I was on leave of absence in Florida, which leave I was spending at St. Petersburg Beach. Having known and served with Major Leslie MacDill in 1918, in France, and hoping to be transferred to MacDill field for duty, I was keenly interested in the establishment of this, the first of the group of new bases to be set up in the long delayed expansion of the Air Corps. The approach to the site of the new base was via what is now MacDill Avenue - then a narrow sand road. My car got stuck in the sand and the last three hundred or so yards leading up to what is now the MacDill Avenue Gate was negotiated by man-power (a group of WPA workers pushing my car this last part of the trip).

From the gate one could see only a vast sweep of scrub pine trees, palmetto growth, and, toward the bay front, low swampy ground. The trees had been felled along the proposed runways, and thru the trees toward the water front could be seen the skeleton frame work of one and two story administration and barrack buildings rising form the sandy swamps. To the layman this would have appeared to be an impossible site for the development of an Air Base. But, having pioneered in early 1917 in the settling and building of Camp Kelly (now Kelly field) Texas, I was not dismayed at the prospects facing those pioneers of MacDill field. In order to be as free as possible from surrounding high obstacles o the approach for landings and the take-off of planes it is always necessary to obtain land for such bases on the outskirts of cities, or at much further distances from them. And, as is always the case in Government purchases, the cost of obtaining the necessary land must be considered.

I was transferred to MacDill Field for duty and arrived there in late March of 1940. The buildings not being ready for occupation at that time the administrative work was being done in offices set up in the City Hall building of Tampa. The senior officer present was then Lt. Colonel H. H. Young, who later assumed command of the now Base, when the first contingent of troops arrived for duty there. The first detachment of troops, commanded by Lieutenant McClellan, arrived in the latter part of April, 1940. This detachment had been sent from Barksdale Field, Louisiana, to form the nucleus from which MacDill field was to start. It was supplemented in May 1940, by additional troops from Barksdale Field, all of which were organized into the 27th Air Base Squadron (later redesignated as the 28th Headquarters and Air Base Squadron, which is today MacDill's Base Unit). This base Squadron was under the command of First Lieutenant John R. (Killer) Kane -- who had brought the second contingent of troops from Barksdale Field.

Now a Colonel, Kane has built up an enviable record to support his nickname of "Killer", which nickname he acquired from him men as a take-off on the comic strip character. Colonel Kane was the first American to bomb Mersa Matruh, and the first to bomb Naples. Hi greatest achievement, however, and for which he received the Congressional Medal of Honor, was as the leader of the third element of heavy bombers which blasted the Ploesti Oil Refineries. These early arrivals were first quartered in the old quarantine area, in tents, until such time as the buildings in the new area were completely ready for occupancy. At that time there were three large main buildings in the quarantine area, plus a few smaller buildings and store houses. At a later date the quarantine area was developed into the present Hospital area, with a great many buildings since added.

When the rainy season set in, about June 1, 1940, it was then discovered just how much of a problem we had to hope to make the base into a livable place. The whole area form the water front to the present Base Headquarters or further was under varying depths of water for weeks at a time. It was a common sight to see as many as fifty or sixty cars bogged down on the sand trails of the Base -- to be towed out by Government trucks or to remain bogged until the rains eased up some. Another sight was to see the Headquarters stenographers brought to the water front near the old Benjamin House (now part of the Officers' Mess) -- there to remove their shoes and socks and wade a quarter of a mile thru mud and water half way to their knees to get to their places of duty. In order to fill in the low spots around and under the buildings trucks hauled sand from the higher spots on the reservation to the building area. The first sidewalks to be placed around the first Headquarters Building were not laid "soft" as is usually done -- they were laid "hard", in sections. These sections were dug from under as much as eighteen inches of water, in the area along the water front and for some distance back. This site had been laid out as a real estate subdivision in the boom days of Florida (in the twenties). Streets had been laid out, gutters and sidewalks put in, and everything made ready for the swarms of people who were going to migrate to Florida from 47 States in the Union. Old time residents told us that though although the expected people didn't come a hurricane did - about 1927 - which drove across Old Tampa Bay onto the present site of MacDill Field, flooding the whole area, and the water rose to such a height that repetition at this time would bring the water to the level of the window bottoms of the present MacDill buildings.)

It was during this first rainy season that a contract was made with a dredging company to start the work of filling in the low areas toward the water front. The work began about August of 1940 and continued until late in 1941. Just how many cubic yards of sand was dredged in from the Bay I could not say, but the work continued until all of the land was well above the Bay water level. The method was to pump the sand from the bottom of the shallow Bay, thru long flexible pipes and hose; the water running off and the remaining sand eventually building up the ground level.

The 29th bombardment Group, first tactical organization at MacDill Field, arrived from Langley Field in May of 1940. The administrative Headquarters were set up at MacDill field, and most of the personnel quartered there. But, as the runways were not yet ready for use the planes operated from Drew Field, which was the old abandoned Tampa Commercial Airport. Tents were set up for Operations, along with sufficient tents for troops to occupy for guard duty, etc., and training of this organization continued at that field until early in January of 1941. MacDill Field had been purchased for a permanent Air Corps Base, but Drew Field was obtained as a sub-base of MacDill field under a 99 year lease. (The City had abandoned Drew Field site where the new Peter O. Knight Field, on Davis Islands, became available for use as a City Airport). As Drew Field was sufficiently suitable for the operation of B-18 bombers, with which the 29th Bombardment Group was then equipped, it was considered advisable to keep that sub-base under lease. (Drew Field has since been enlarged to the extent that all types of planes operate safely thereat.)

With the activation of new Groups, by splitting up the old 29th Group and using "key" men with long service in the Air Corps - and adding new recruits to same, the 3rd Bombardment Wing was organized, under the command of General Tinker. This set-up brought an administrative difficulties - as the Base Commander was, under Army Regulations which had not in the years gone by been formulated with such a set-up in view, responsible for the administration and discipline of the Base, but the Tactical Commander, who was the senior to the Base Commander, had his troops on the same Base. The Base Commander's duties were purely administrative - he was to provide security for the Base, maintenance and discipline, as well as to provide facilities to enable the Tactical Commander to fulfill his functions. The Tactical Commander's chief duty was to ensure the tactical training and readiness of his organizations for action - but, in the performance of this he had to have certain administrative functions. This situation led to some misunderstanding - honest conflict of opinion as to just where one Commander's responsibility and authority stopped and the other commander's started. After several months of operating under these difficulties higher authority issued instructions to the effect that Bases where Wing Commanders established their headquarters would be commanded by that Wing Commander. The Base Commander thus became the Executive Officer for the Base, under the Tactical Commander. This ironed out the former administrative difficulties - the Wing Commander having a Tactical Staff and a Base Staff. (But, at a later date the Wings were done away with - and what had been called Wings now became Bomber Commands, fighter Commanders, etc. With this charge in designations higher authority apparently overlooked the principle earlier establishing authority in Tactical Commanders over Bases whereat they established their Headquarters).

In answer to the question as to duties performed by the Engineer Officer on the Staff: Lt. Colonel Roy S. Burdick, C.N., was on General Tinker's Staff. His duties were, in addition to keeping the General informed on matters pertaining to Engineering activities on the Base (not to be confused with the activities of the Air Corps Base Engineering functions), to be on Boards or Committees designated to inspect sites for proposed outlying bombing ranges, etc. The sites were picked by Air Corps Officers from the air - then the Board (or committee) would be required to proceed overland or water to the selected site, to inspect and report upon its desirability, availability, etc. In the event that it was contemplated installing any utilities thereat a Quartermaster Officer would be on the Board or Committee. The Air Corps Officer would consider the desirability of the site from the flying standpoint - the Engineer Officer from the construction standpoint - and the Quartermaster from the standpoint of desired or planned installation of utilities - the whole Board as to the availability of the site, rental, etc.

Shortly after Pearl Harbor there was established at MacDill Field a Ferry Command. This station was established as the "jumping off" spot for certain selected personnel and materials to be sent to the Far East. It was done with all possible secrecy - the planes took off at night, flew to a South American Port - thence across the South Atlantic, across Central Africa, thru the Middle East and on to the Far East. The project was a well kept secret - no one but those directly responsible knew what personnel and materials were sent on these flights, or what their exact destinations were.

Having started to fly in 1912, I enlisted in the Aviation Section of the Signal corps on April 12, 1917 - six days after War was declared. I arrived at Camp Kelly (now Kelly Field) in May, and was on my way to France in August. I received my primary Military Flying Training at Tours, France with the French, getting my pilot wings and commission as a Reserve Officer in May of 1918. I then was transferred to Issoudon, France, for advanced flying training which was under American supervision. After 22 months overseas I returned to the states, and was stationed at Mitchell Field for five months. In late 1919 I was transferred to Maxwell Field where, on July 1, 1920, I was commissioned in the Regular Army Air Corps. My next station was Crissy Field where I was stationed form 1922 to 1927. From 1927 to 1929 I was on duty with the Alabama National Guard Air Service. From 1929 to 1931 I served at Marshall Field, For Riley, Kansas. then from 1931 to 1936 I commanded Lawson Field, For Benning, Georgia. In 1936 I was ordered to the Philippines. During my first four months there I had command of the 28th Bombardment Squadron, at Nichols Field, on the outskirts of Manila. Thereafter, I commanded Clark Field, Fort Stotsenburg, which is sixty miles North of Manila. During my tour of command of Clark Field I was sent to Japan for a tour of duty inspecting Japanese aviation activities and making economic surveys. Upon my return to the States, in 1938, I was stationed at Langley Field - until my transfer to MacDill Field, in early 1940. I was retired in 1942 because of physical disability in line of duty.